INSIDE

MONSTER GARAGE™

WRITTEN BY KEN VOSE

MEREDITH® BOOKS
DES MOINES, IOWA

Writer: Ken Vose
Book Design by: Matthew Eberhart
Senior Associate Design Director: John Seid
Cover Photographers: F. Scott Schafer (Jesse James); John Bramley (crew)
Contributing Photographers: John Bramley, Dave Lindsay,
    Beatrice Neumann, Rick Scherer, Steve Bonge, Rahoul Ghose,
    Cat Gwynn, Chris Hildreth, Virginia Lee Hunter, Clint Karlsen,
    Daniel Lincoln, Clay McLachlan, David McNew,
    Gilles Mingasson, Gary Payne, Peter Taylor
Contributing Illustrators: Wayne Bjerke (Utility Vehicles and Municipal
    Vehicles); Steve Vandervate (Recreational Vehicles)
Copy Chief: Terri Fredrickson
Copy and Production Editor: Victoria Forlini
Editorial Operations Manager: Karen Schirm
Managers, Book Production: Pam Kvitne,
    Marjorie J. Schenkelberg, Rick Vonholdt
Contributing Researcher: Cheryl Alkon
Contributing Copy Editor: Lori Blachford
Contributing Proofreaders: David Craft, Gretchen Kauffman
Electronic Production Coordinator: Paula Forest
Editorial and Design Assistants: Kaye Chabot,
    Patty Loder, Karen McFadden, Mary Lee Gavin

Meredith Books
Editor in Chief: Linda Raglan Cunningham
Design Director: Matt Strelecki
Executive Editor, New Business Development: Dan Rosenberg

Publisher: James D. Blume
Executive Director, Marketing: Jeffrey Myers
Executive Director, New Business Development: Todd M. Davis
Executive Director, Sales: Ken Zagor
Director, Operations: George A. Susral
Director, Production: Douglas M. Johnston
Business Director: Jim Leonard

Vice President and General Manager: Douglas J. Guendel

Meredith Publishing Group
President, Publishing Group: Stephen M. Lacy
Vice President-Publishing Director: Bob Mate

Meredith Corporation
Chairman and Chief Executive Officer: William T. Kerr

In Memoriam: E. T. Meredith III (1933–2003)

KEN VOSE, the writer for INSIDE MONSTER GARAGE, is a former race driver. He is the author of *The Car: Past & Present, The Convertible,* and *Blue Guitar.* He has also written two novels set in the world of Formula One racing (*Oversteer* and *Dead Pedal*) and is the coauthor of the book and screenplay *Greased Lightning.*

MONSTER GARAGE BOOK DEVELOPMENT TEAM
Thom Beers, Executive Producer, Original Productions
Clark Bunting II, General Manager, Discovery Channel
Sharon M. Bennett, Senior Vice President, Strategic
    Partnerships & Licensing
Deirdre Scott, Vice President, Licensing
Carol LeBlanc, Vice President, Marketing & Retail Development
Sean Gallagher, Director of Programming Development,
    Discovery Channel
Elizabeth Bakacs, Creative Director, Strategic Partnerships
Erica Jacobs Green, Publishing Manager

All of us at Meredith Books are dedicated to providing you with information and ideas to enhance your life. We welcome your comments and suggestions. Write to us at: Meredith Books, New Business Development Department, 1716 Locust St., Des Moines, IA 50309-3023.

If you would like to purchase any Meredith Books home, family, or lifestyle titles, check wherever quality books are sold. Or visit us at: meredithbooks.com

The original manufacturers of the vehicles, parts, and accessories appearing in this book in no way sponsor, endorse, or are otherwise affiliated with this book, the Monster Garage series, or Discovery Communications, Inc. All vehicle makes and models are trademarks of the respective manufacturers.

WHAT'S INSIDE

MONSTER GARAGE™

SET TOUR

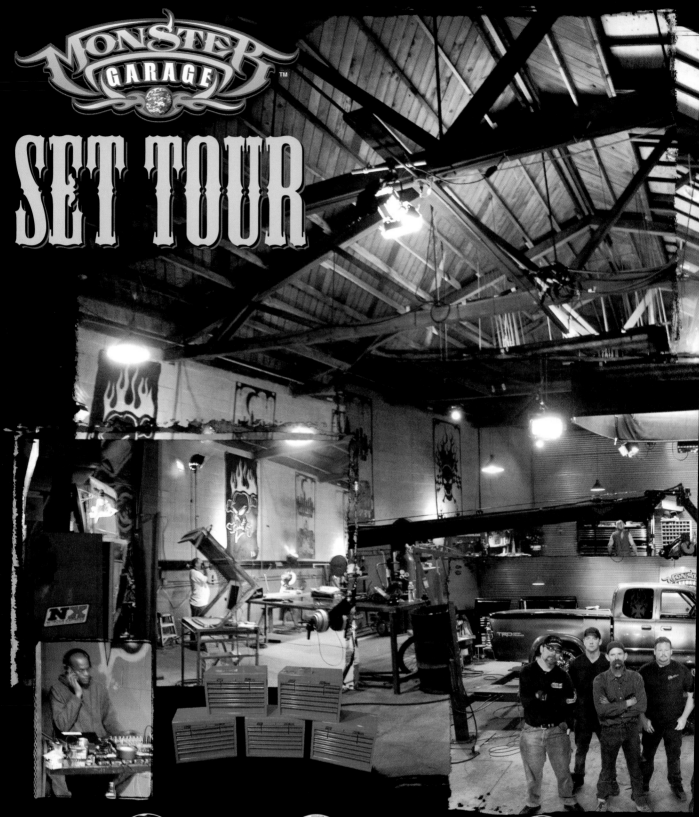

MONSTER TOOLS

AS EXPLAINED
BY GARAGE
MANAGER
ALEX ANDERSON

TIG WELDER

TIG means tungsten inert gas. A small portable argon gas unit used primarily for welding aluminum and stainless steel alloys. It's hard to use until you get it down, but it's very clean and excellent for jobs that require smaller, more precise welding. It's what Jesse uses on his special exhaust systems.

OXYACETYLENE TORCH

A gas cutting outfit that's kind of old-school, not high-tech. It puts out a really hot flame. Plasma cutters have replaced most of the fire cutting instruments. It's a torch that will cut metal tubing, a chassis frame, practically anything. It will weld steel or brass. It's also used to clean tar or anything else off of metal surfaces by heating it up, and then you scrape it off. It's used here a lot to heat steel up in order to bend it.

650 PLASMA CUTTER

This uses an electric arc process to cut through stainless steel, carbon steel, sheet metal, aluminum, just about anything in the shop. It will cut through $5/8$-inch-thick metal. The process uses a concentrated electrical arc that melts the material through a high-temperature plasma beam.

MONSTER GARAGE
RULES

1. When built, the monster machine must appear to be stock. The team can spend no more than $3,000 in cold cash for parts.

2. Jesse and his crew have seven days and nights. On the first day they design. For the next five, they build. And on the seventh day, they race.

3. If successful, each team member walks away with a $3,400 set of Mac tools, and the clock starts... now!

MIG WELDER
MIG means metal inert gas. The MIG has a continuous wire feed which also helps to conduct electricity. There is a spool of wire inside it, and when you pull the trigger, it feeds it out. When you make contact with a piece of clean metal, you create a ground and you can start to weld. The gas inside is argon, which is nonflammable and used as a flux. We use a 75/25 steel mix here, which is argon and carbon monoxide mixed together. It's cheaper than using straight argon.

LIQUID-COOLED TIG WELDER
This unit is water cooled so you can weld for longer periods of time without it overheating.

CHOP SAW
An abrasive saw that will cut through metal. The blade is primarily composed of fiberglass and sand sandwiched together.

TUBE BENDER
As its name implies, it's used for bending steel tubing and shaping sheet metal.

DISC SANDER
This is probably the handiest piece of equipment in the shop. It can shape or grind down practically anything.

ENGLISH WHEEL
The English wheel is used for shaping sheet metal. It's particularly useful for forming compound curves.

5

MONSTER GARAGE™

RECREATIONAL VEHICLES

SCHOOL BUS PONTOON BOAT

MINI COOPER SNOW MOBILE

WINNE BAGO SKATE RAMP

GEO TRACKER HOT AIR BALLOON

It drives, it floats, it's the
PARTY SKOOL

" My idea was to make it like a tackle box. You split it and the sides rotate down and become the pontoons. "

JESSE JAMES

THE MISSION: TAKE A 20-PASSENGER SCHOOL BUS AND TURN IT INTO THE ULTIMATE PARTY BOAT

SKOOL BUS

TEAM

JESSE JAMES

CHARLIE CONN, JR.
Bus technician
RIVERSIDE, CALIFORNIA

JIM DAY
Sculptor and fabricator
INGLEWOOD, CALIFORNIA

STEVE FURNISH
Fabricator
LONG BEACH, CALIFORNIA

ROB KING
Boat designer
EL CAJON, CALIFORNIA

TOM PREWITT
Custom painter
BREA, CALIFORNIA

DARREN SHURIG
Engineering fabricator
FOUNTAIN VALLEY, CALIFORNIA

JOHN WEST
Boat builder and designer
EL CAJON, CALIFORNIA

SPECS

VEHICLE
1989 Ford 20-passenger school bus.
Height: 7 feet 10 inches.
Width: 7 feet. Length: 24 feet.
Weight: 14,150 pounds (7 tons)

ENGINE
Stock 351 Cleveland V-8 Ford

TRANSMISSION
Stock C-6 Ford

SUSPENSION-
BRAKES-STEERING
Stock Ford

PAINT
By House of Kolor. Chrome yellow
base covered with sunshine pearl
and coated with ice pearl.

WHEELS
KMC

MONSTER SPECS
Propeller attached to shaft under
the bus; internal winch utilizing
pulleys and steel cables to lower
each pontoon down to the side once
it is lifted by four actuators; foam
to fill the pontoons.

THE BUILD

MONSTER

In 1939 the official color for school buses was changed from Omaha orange to chrome yellow.

FACTOID

" *I would rate this as out there on the wacky meter. I'm sure there are crazier ideas, but this is out there; it's in the top ten.* "

CHARLIE CONN, JR.

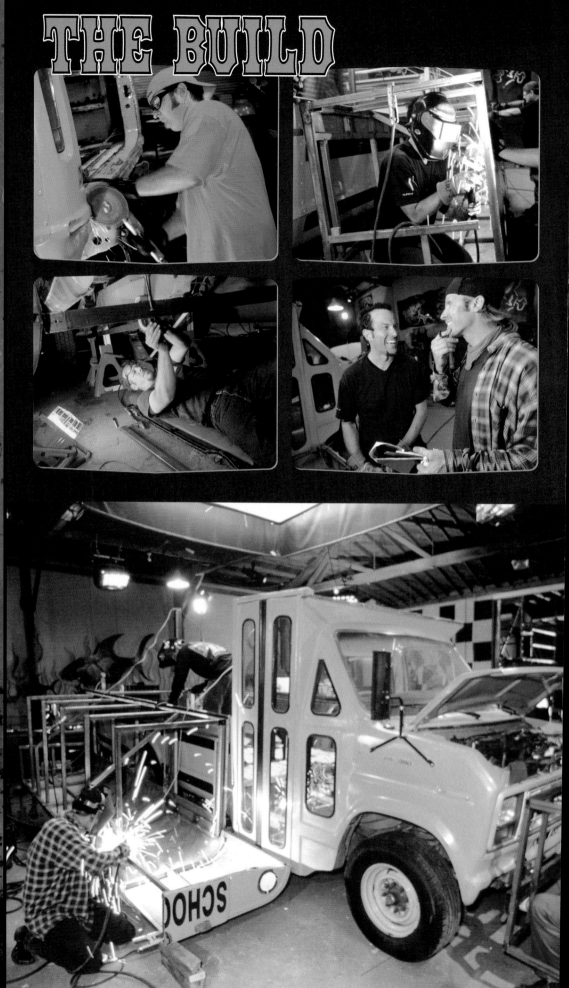

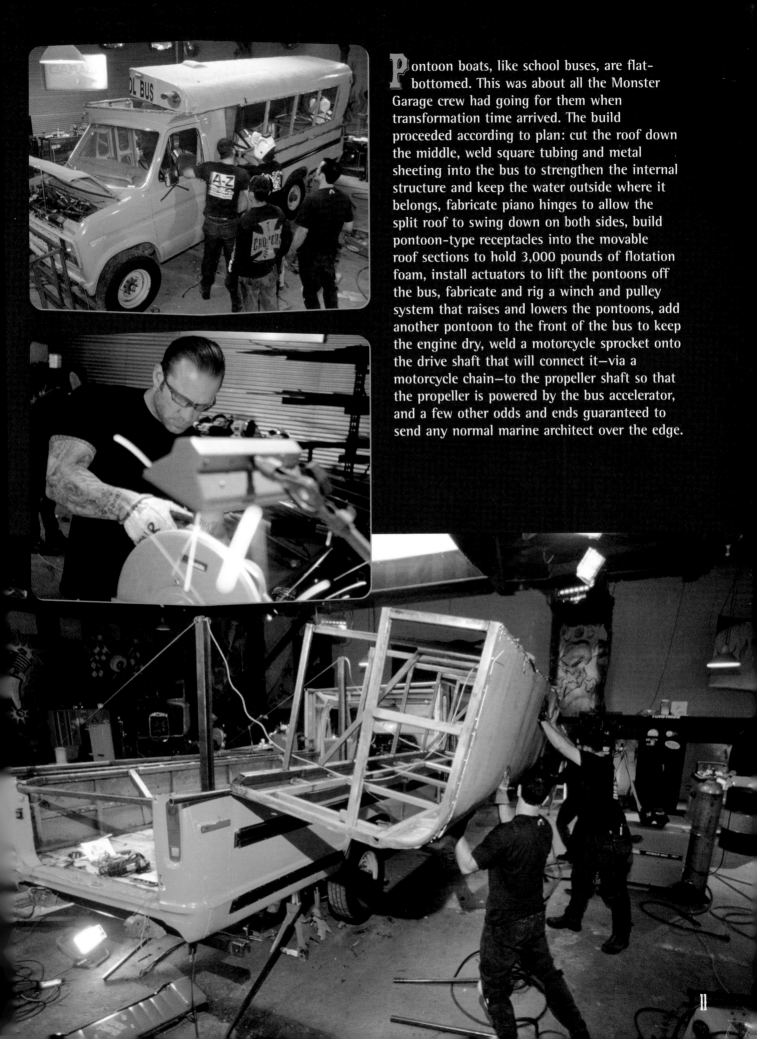

Pontoon boats, like school buses, are flat-bottomed. This was about all the Monster Garage crew had going for them when transformation time arrived. The build proceeded according to plan: cut the roof down the middle, weld square tubing and metal sheeting into the bus to strengthen the internal structure and keep the water outside where it belongs, fabricate piano hinges to allow the split roof to swing down on both sides, build pontoon-type receptacles into the movable roof sections to hold 3,000 pounds of flotation foam, install actuators to lift the pontoons off the bus, fabricate and rig a winch and pulley system that raises and lowers the pontoons, add another pontoon to the front of the bus to keep the engine dry, weld a motorcycle sprocket onto the drive shaft that will connect it—via a motorcycle chain—to the propeller shaft so that the propeller is powered by the bus accelerator, and a few other odds and ends guaranteed to send any normal marine architect over the edge.

> **"** *Our boats are all fiberglass boats— mostly performance boats, but we have some experience with pontoon-style boats; they're more like minivans or station wagons, whereas the boats we build are more like Porsches or Ferraris. This boat is way out there. We've built several thousand boats but nothing like this. We never dreamed of doing anything like this before.*
>
> *"All guys want to change or modify things, you know, make things faster. Nothing is ever good enough as it sits. You never take a car and just leave it alone. You've got to put some rims on it or change something. It's a signature of yourself when you customize something; whether it's a car or a boat, it says a little bit about yourself.* **"**

JOHN WEST

The team arrives at Lake Havasu to take on a 25-foot pontoon boat in a race in which points are scored for speed, navigation, and the ability to fire up a barbecue grill in a mild breeze. The Monster Garage team wins the day when the crew of the other boat abandons ship to join our merry pranksters on the bus.

MONSTER

There are currently at least 27 rock 'n' roll songs about buses.

FACTOID

JESSE'S FINAL THOUGHTS

"That one was just hard because of the sheer amount of labor. Doing such a big thing took a six-guy crew. It was a big project."

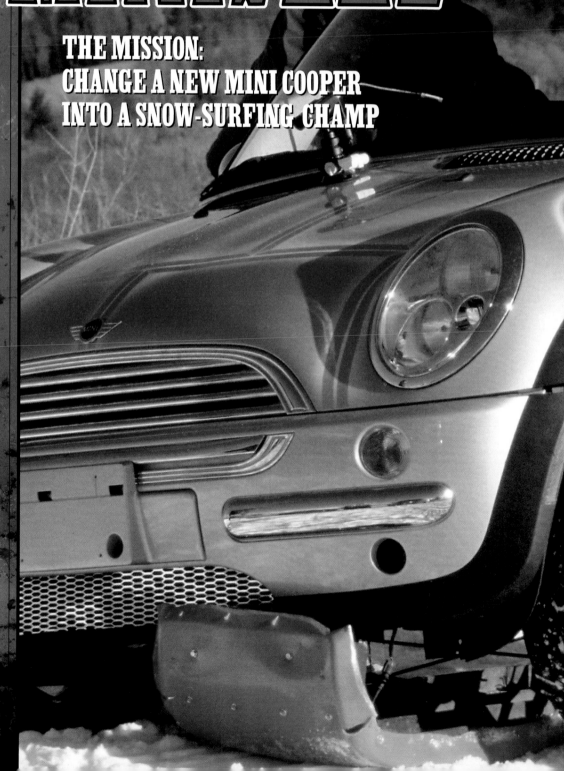

Chairlift not required

MINISLED

THE MISSION:
CHANGE A NEW MINI COOPER
INTO A SNOW-SURFING CHAMP

MINI COOPER SNOW MOBILE

> "I have zero experience on snow; never been skiing or snowboarding. It's cold."

JESSE JAMES

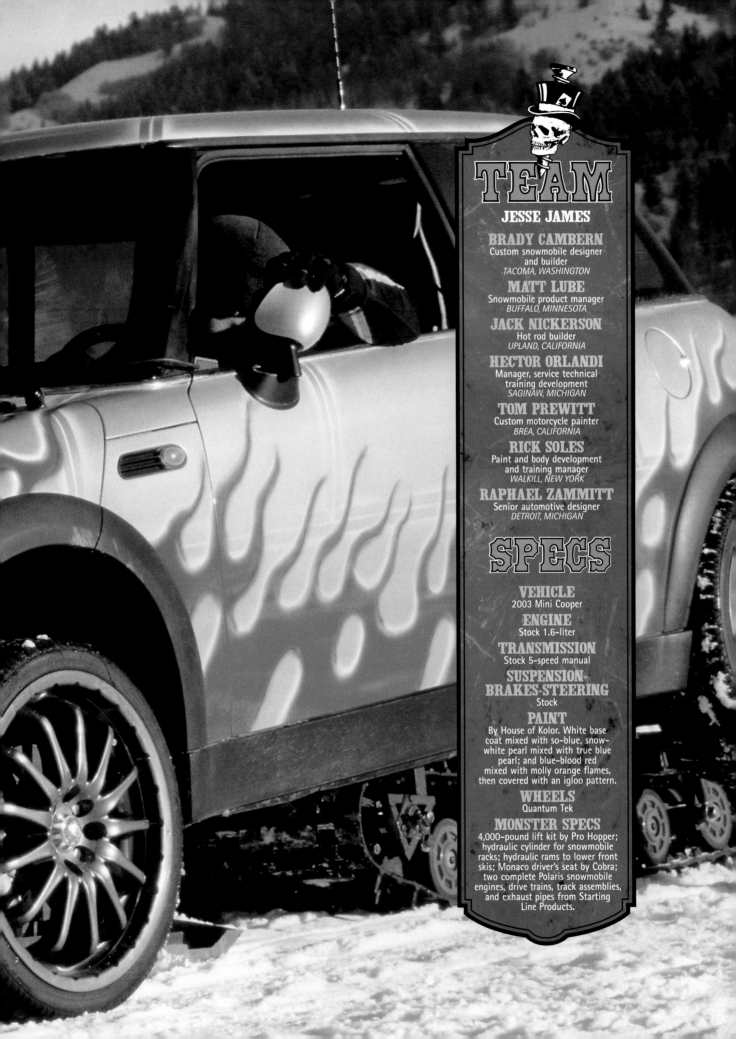

TEAM

JESSE JAMES

BRADY CAMBERN
Custom snowmobile designer
and builder
TACOMA, WASHINGTON

MATT LUBE
Snowmobile product manager
BUFFALO, MINNESOTA

JACK NICKERSON
Hot rod builder
UPLAND, CALIFORNIA

HECTOR ORLANDI
Manager, service technical
training development
SAGINAW, MICHIGAN

TOM PREWITT
Custom motorcycle painter
BREA, CALIFORNIA

RICK SOLES
Paint and body development
and training manager
WALKILL, NEW YORK

RAPHAEL ZAMMITT
Senior automotive designer
DETROIT, MICHIGAN

SPECS

VEHICLE
2003 Mini Cooper

ENGINE
Stock 1.6-liter

TRANSMISSION
Stock 5-speed manual

**SUSPENSION-
BRAKES-STEERING**
Stock

PAINT
By House of Kolor. White base
coat mixed with so-blue, snow-
white pearl mixed with true blue
pearl; and blue-blood red
mixed with molly orange flames,
then covered with an igloo pattern.

WHEELS
Quantum Tek

MONSTER SPECS
4,000-pound lift kit by Pro Hopper;
hydraulic cylinder for snowmobile
racks; hydraulic rams to lower front
skis; Monaco driver's seat by Cobra;
two complete Polaris snowmobile
engines, drive trains, track assemblies,
and exhaust pipes from Starting
Line Products.

We've got to put ten pounds of stuff in a five-pound bag.

JACK NICKERSON

THE BUILD

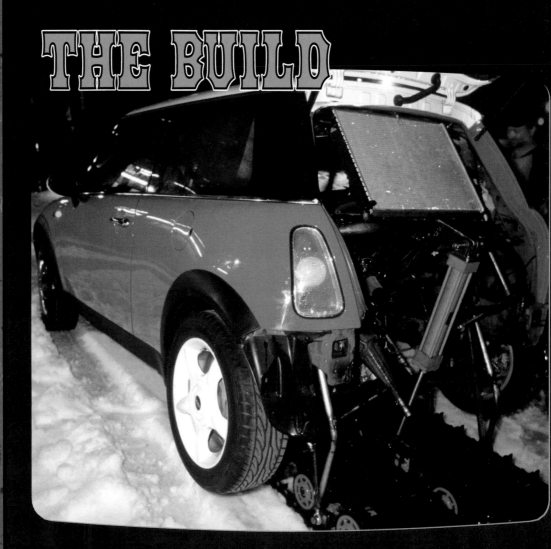

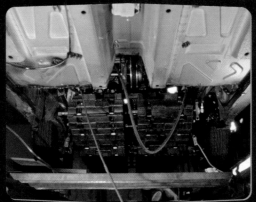

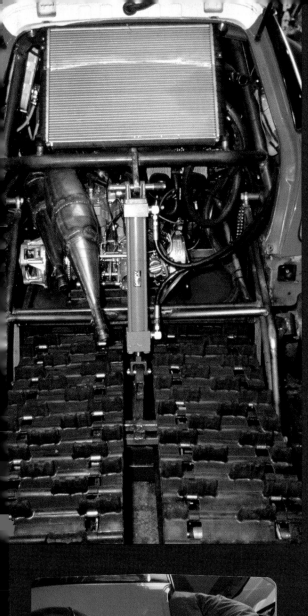

The interior of the Mini would have to be more than gutted to make room for two 140-horsepower Polaris snowmobile engines and two snowmobile tracks. A stock snowmobile track is eighteen inches high. These would need to be half that size. The idea was to make the two engines and tracks as one 600-pound unit that could then be inserted into the back of the Mini.

Hector Orlandi conceives and builds the eponymous "Hector Stick," a contraption that will allow Jesse to power each engine with one lever. The weight of the combined engine-and-track unit proves too much for the Mini's unibody frame. Jesse builds a reinforced cage with 2-inch tubing to support the extra weight. A four-link system that attaches to the cage is fabricated. It connects to the track unit, allowing it to swing in and out of the back of the car. Front skis are fabricated from $1/8$-inch steel plates. They will be raised and lowered by two actuators.

When the engines arrive they are assembled and fitted onto the engine mount on the tracks. The unit is then shoehorned into the back of the car and attached to the four-link set up. Jesse wants a hydraulic ram installed to raise and lower the unit onto the snow.

Day Five turns into a full 24-hour day. The crew pulls an all-nighter to ensure that the job will be completed by midnight of the following day. The biggest problem is with the hydraulic ram and pump that raise and lower the 600-pound track unit. After inspecting the installation of Swamp Buggy, which is parked in another section of the garage, a solution is found and, at about 5 a.m., the ram does its job. Everyone staggers out to shower and get a few minutes' sleep before the final Day Six push—everyone but Brady Cambern, who stays to complete the fabrication of the engine exhaust pipes.

The final day proves a long one, but by 11 p.m. everything is working to everyone's satisfaction. Jesse brings the crew and Mini over to a parking lot where, to the amazement of the citizens of Long Beach, the surface is covered with snow. The Mini does its thing. Bring on "The King."

THE CHALLENGE

If it had wheels and I had one, I wanted to race somebody that had another one.

RICK SOLES

The challenge takes place in Alpine, Wyoming. Jesse and the Monster Mini will have to go head-to-head with Richard Petty and his 130-horsepower, 100-plus-miles-per-hour Polaris 700 ProX2. The Mini holds its own, but the combination of the high-powered and lightweight Polaris driven by "The King" is just too much for the Mini to handle.

JESSE'S FINAL THOUGHTS

"That was cool, but it was hard. It was the closest one coming to not making it. It was cool racing Richard. I knew when I went up there we were gonna race. Before we even realized that the snowmobile was way faster than the Mini, I realized that no matter what, he couldn't lose; he's The King."

This half-pipe is gonna roll

OLLIE HOTEL

WINNEBAGO SKATE RAMP

THE MISSION:
TURN A WINNEBAGO
MOTOR HOME INTO A RADICAL
ROLLING MONSTER HALF-PIPE

" *It's just going to be a whole lot of labor.* "

JESSE JAMES

TEAM

JESSE JAMES

CHRIS ARTIAGA
Skateboarder and fabricator
SAN LUIS OBISPO, CALIFORNIA

NIGEL BENJAMIN
Master carpenter
TOLUCA LAKE, CALIFORNIA

STEVE CADENA
Creative consultant
LONG BEACH, CALIFORNIA

TONY HAWK
Pro skater
SAN JUAN CAPISTRANO, CALIFORNIA

JASON JESSEE
Pro skater and motorcycle fabricator
SANTA CRUZ, CALIFORNIA

JEFF KING
Skate-rail and ramp builder
SAN DIEGO, CALIFORNIA

JOE MCCLUSKEY
Custom-car builder
HEMET, CALIFORNIA

MIKE MCINTYRE
Skate-ramp engineer and builder
TEMPE, ARIZONA

RICK THORNE
Professional BMX freestyler
SANTA ANA, CALIFORNIA

SPECS

VEHICLE
1987 Winnebago Itasca Suncruiser

ENGINE
Stock 464 Industrial

TRANSMISSION
Stock 3-speed automatic C-6

SUSPENSION– BRAKES–STEERING
Firestone Ride-Rite leaf springs.
Stock brakes and power steering.

PAINT
By House of Kolor. Spray paint
by James Real and Ken Cassidy.

WHEELS
Stock

MONSTER SPECS
20 sheets of $^1/_2$-inch by 10-foot
plywood, 10 sheets of $^1/_4$-inch by
10-foot ramp armor,
32 pieces of 1$^1/_2$-inch tubing.

MONSTER

In the 1950s, some California surfers put wheels on wood and started "Sidewalk Surfing." Skateboarding was born.

FACTOID

" I love the smell of metal when it's burning. "
STEVE CADENA

THE BUILD

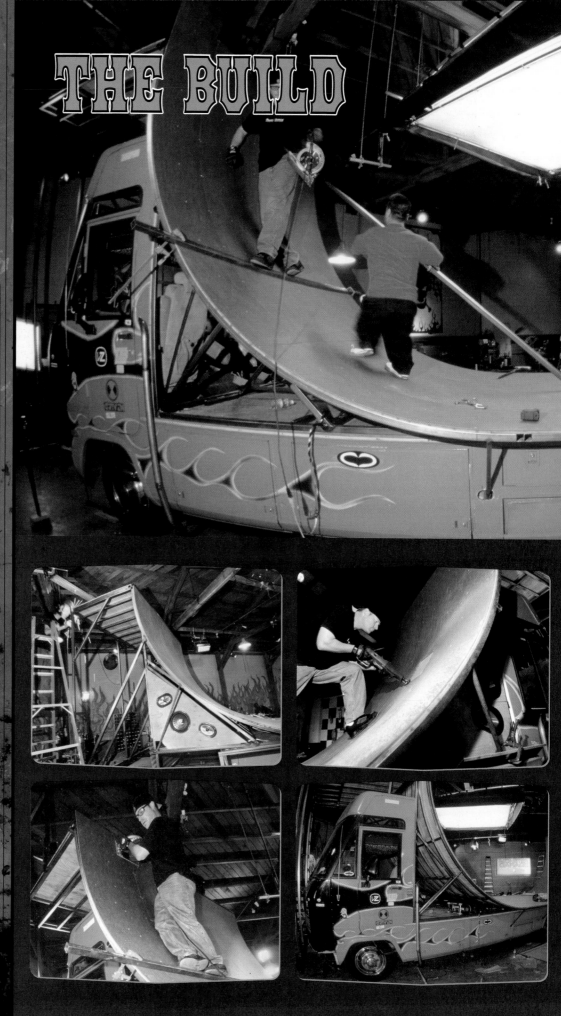

The eight-man build team begins by destroying the "home" part of the motor home to make room for the half-pipe framework. Almost immediately a glitch comes up on the radar screen. The twelve-foot-wide ramp mandated by the design team will work fine, provided the ramp never has to leave the garage: The exit door is only eleven feet wide. The quick answer is to lop off two feet and keep building. Steel tubing is bought, cut to length, shaped, and positioned on the bed of the RV.

The next glitch arises on Day Two when Nigel must have decided that things had ceased being fun, because at that point he takes a permanent walk. The team forges ahead, fabricating and securing the front and back decks to the ramp structure. The plywood arrives and is put in place without a problem, which leads to yet another glitch: Jeff, upset that the logo of one of his competitors appears on the wooden ramp (which they had donated), takes a can of spray paint and covers it over. Series producer Tom McMahon lets Jeff know what he thinks of that, and once the two finish their discussions, Jeff, too, takes a walk, albeit not a permanent one. The team is shrinking, but the ramp continues to grow.

On the last day, with every section snugly secured and smooth as can be, the team installs a giant stereo system organized by Jesse and pulls the monster out into the Long Beach night. It is a monumental example of the Monster Garage mantra: If you can't hear it before you can see it, then what's the point? The ramp moves, the skaters skate, the monster lives.

THE CHALLENGE

24

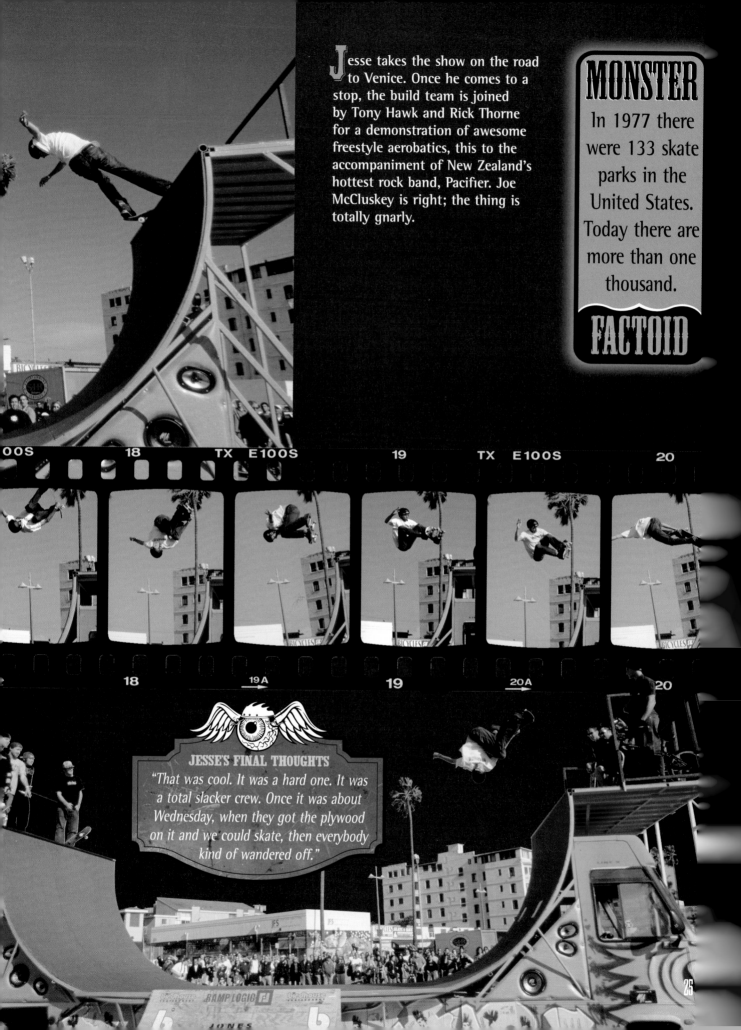

Jesse takes the show on the road to Venice. Once he comes to a stop, the build team is joined by Tony Hawk and Rick Thorne for a demonstration of awesome freestyle aerobatics, this to the accompaniment of New Zealand's hottest rock band, Pacifier. Joe McCluskey is right; the thing is totally gnarly.

MONSTER

In 1977 there were 133 skate parks in the United States. Today there are more than one thousand.

FACTOID

JESSE'S FINAL THOUGHTS

"That was cool. It was a hard one. It was a total slacker crew. Once it was about Wednesday, when they got the plywood on it and we could skate, then everybody kind of wandered off."

GEO TRACKER HOT AIR BALLOON

" *Just the wrongness of it is what makes it good.* "

JESSE JAMES

Jesse and the Geo take the very high road

HOT AIR RIDE

THE MISSION: TAKE A GEO TRACKER WHERE NONE HAD GONE BEFORE

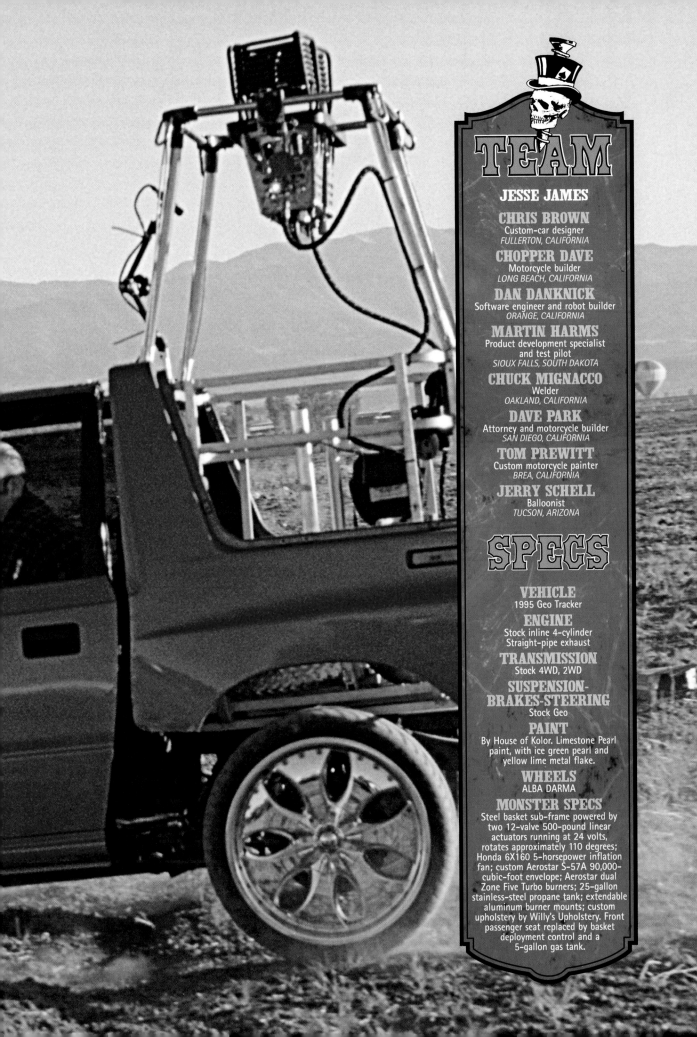

TEAM

JESSE JAMES

CHRIS BROWN
Custom-car designer
FULLERTON, CALIFORNIA

CHOPPER DAVE
Motorcycle builder
LONG BEACH, CALIFORNIA

DAN DANKNICK
Software engineer and robot builder
ORANGE, CALIFORNIA

MARTIN HARMS
Product development specialist
and test pilot
SIOUX FALLS, SOUTH DAKOTA

CHUCK MIGNACCO
Welder
OAKLAND, CALIFORNIA

DAVE PARK
Attorney and motorcycle builder
SAN DIEGO, CALIFORNIA

TOM PREWITT
Custom motorcycle painter
BREA, CALIFORNIA

JERRY SCHELL
Balloonist
TUCSON, ARIZONA

SPECS

VEHICLE
1995 Geo Tracker

ENGINE
Stock inline 4-cylinder
Straight-pipe exhaust

TRANSMISSION
Stock 4WD, 2WD

SUSPENSION-BRAKES-STEERING
Stock Geo

PAINT
By House of Kolor. Limestone Pearl
paint, with ice green pearl and
yellow lime metal flake.

WHEELS
ALBA DARMA

MONSTER SPECS
Steel basket sub-frame powered by
two 12-valve 500-pound linear
actuators running at 24 volts,
rotates approximately 110 degrees;
Honda 6X160 5-horsepower inflation
fan; custom Aerostar S-57A 90,000-
cubic-foot envelope; Aerostar dual
Zone Five Turbo burners; 25-gallon
stainless-steel propane tank; extendable
aluminum burner mounts; custom
upholstery by Willy's Upholstery. Front
passenger seat replaced by basket
deployment control and a
5-gallon gas tank.

THE BUILD

MONSTER

The first recorded fuel used in a hot-air balloon in 1783 was old boots and bad meat. The stink was thought to increase the buoyancy.

FACTOID

I think this is going to be a monstrous vehicle. It's on fire basically. I think it's going to be a little scarier than just your typical rainbow-colored balloon.

CHRIS BROWN

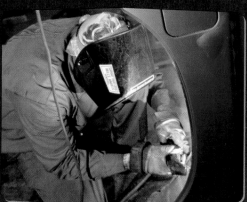

Cars are heavy. Hot-air balloons are light. The weight of the balloon, fuel tank, fuel, burners, and two passengers would be approximately 950 pounds. With a calculated maximum lift of 1,650 pounds this would limit the weight of the basket to a maximum of 600 pounds. This elemental problem is solved by the team stripping off all excess parts, which included cutting off the entire back half of the Tracker. All nonessential steel is stripped from the rear and a steel sub-frame, suggested by Jesse, is fabricated and installed. The sub-frame tilts the basket back to inflate the envelope (that's balloonspeak for the balloon), then tilts back up as the heated air fills the balloon and, finally, releases the basket for

flight. The all-aluminum basket must meet FAA standards. Two 500-pound linear actuators powered by two Hawker 12-volt gel cells from Team Delta take care of the tilting while a Jesse-designed pin-and-spring assembly handles the basket release. To meet FAA requirements, additional supports are added and the top horizontal support lowered. The completed basket weighs in at 190 pounds.

Finally, it's time for the all-important test lift-off. The assembly tilts and releases perfectly. The nineteen-million-BTU burners roar to life, shooting twenty-foot flames into the night skies over Long Beach. In a scene worthy of Jules Verne, Jesse and the Tracker take to the sky.

" Ballooning has been around for more than 200 years, starting in France back in 1783. It was the earliest form of manned flight. There are probably four to five thousand active balloon pilots flying in the U.S. today.

"There's nothing quite like the freedom of floating. When I used to do passenger rides, I'd get a lot of people in the basket that were looking for a thrill ride, like a roller coaster or a parachute jump, but it's nothing like that. When you take off it's a smooth, gentle event as you leave the ground and float free with the wind, not really knowing where the wind is going to take you. "

MARTIN HARMS

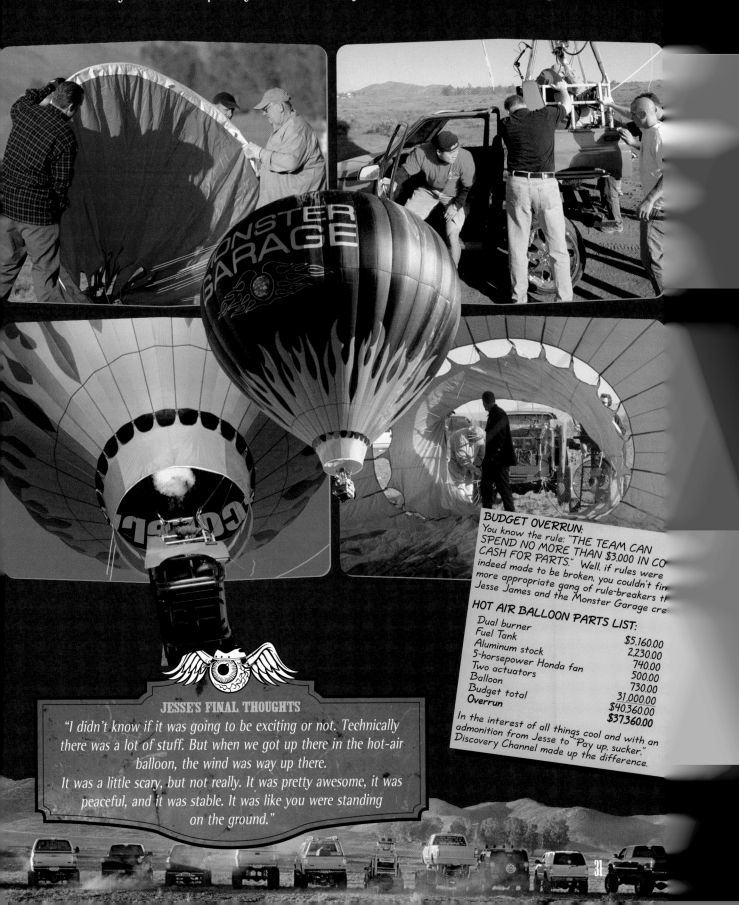

Jesse and the Geo take on a gaggle of off-road machines on a 7.2-mile course laid out in the Southern California desert. At first the off-roadies have the upper hand, but once the balloon is inflated, Jesse and the Geo take the high road, soaring serenely to what will prove yet another victory for the forces of Monster Garage.

BUDGET OVERRUN:

You know the rule: "THE TEAM CAN SPEND NO MORE THAN $3,000 IN CO CASH FOR PARTS." Well, if rules were indeed made to be broken, you couldn't fin more appropriate gang of rule-breakers th Jesse James and the Monster Garage cre

HOT AIR BALLOON PARTS LIST:

Dual burner	
Fuel Tank	$5,160.00
Aluminum stock	2,230.00
5-horsepower Honda fan	740.00
Two actuators	500.00
Balloon	730.00
Budget total	31,000.00
Overrun	$40,360.00
	$37,360.00

In the interest of all things cool and with an admonition from Jesse to "Pay up, sucker," Discovery Channel made up the difference.

JESSE'S FINAL THOUGHTS

"I didn't know if it was going to be exciting or not. Technically there was a lot of stuff. But when we got up there in the hot-air balloon, the wind was way up there.
It was a little scary, but not really. It was pretty awesome, it was peaceful, and it was stable. It was like you were standing on the ground."

A GUY NAMED THOM

TURNING A DREAM INTO REALITY

Do you ever wonder where the idea for a play, a movie, or a television program comes from? In the case of Monster Garage, one of the most successful shows on cable television, the idea came about because somebody literally dreamed it up.

"Dreams have always been a big part of my life," says Thom Beers, President and Executive Producer of Original Productions and Creator of the Monster Garage series. "I remember having them back when I worked for Ted Turner as Vice President of Turner Original Productions. I was in my late thirties and I'd been with Turner for eleven years supervising *National Geographic Explorer* and the *Jacques Cousteau Specials* when I started having these weird dreams, that one day I'd wake up and I was fifty years old and just handed a pink slip. An out-of-work middle-aged TV guy in Atlanta—that's not a bad dream, that's a nightmare! My dreams were deferred when Paramount hired me to move to California and produce a new wildlife series, *Wild Things,* with *Cops* producer Bertram van Munster. Sure enough, seven months later my teammates at Turner got a wake-up call when the new Time Warner management group shut down that entire unit.

"Monster Garage came about much the same way. After a heavy steak dinner I woke up in the middle of the night and said out loud, 'Oh yeah,' then went back to sleep. I didn't remember it at all until my wife, Leslie, asked me about it the next morning. Thank God she reminded me. It was this weird dream—this Mustang belching fire and spitting dirt, literally turned into a lawnmower, and I started thinking about transformations. That's what people are fascinated by. And they are fascinated with going back to the basics, about doing stuff with your hands."

Having the dream is one thing. Turning it into a hit series is a Mustang of another color. At the time Monster Garage was beginning to take shape, Beers recently had produced two successful programs for The Discovery Channel about the world of custom motorcycles: *Motorcycle Mania* and *Motorcycle Mania II.* "I'd already done the definitive *History of Harley* for Turner Broadcasting," he says, "so I started looking for something else. The guys at *Easyriders* magazine gave my producer, Hugh King, the names of custom chopper builders from all over the West Coast, and Jesse James was on the list. We visited about twenty places before we went to West Coast Choppers. It was the ultimate playground: The showroom was filled with beautiful custom-built choppers, low riders, a chopped and channeled '49 Ford Truck—not to mention a 700-gallon fish tank with live sharks in it. The workshop had grinders, lathes, power hammers, band saws, welders, sparks flying, urban and metal music blaring. It was like I died and went to boy heaven. Then I met Jesse. He was thoughtful, very bright, and totally bad."

"Then it all started to click," Beers continues. My executive producer at The Discovery Channel had called me to tell me that they were looking for something kind of like TLC's *Junkyard Wars.* They had already taken a number of pitches

from producers when I came in and pitched them my transformation dream. They decided to give it a shot. All of a sudden it all fell into place—a show where guys do nearly the impossible by transforming a car into something outrageous by using their own hands. We got lucky, because not only was it a really good idea, but we also found a really good host with Jesse.

"I went to Jesse and asked if he wanted to be the host. He immediately got it and signed on. The cool thing is selling a new series, the tough thing is making it. We had to go out and actually create a working garage, stock it with tools, and find talented builders, fabricators, and mechanics. I remember going to car shows and swap meets trying to get people on board. Telling a grown man that we wanted to turn a Mustang into a lawnmower elicited an interesting reaction. There would be this long pause, and then the question. 'Why?' The guys we cast, most of them were the ones who said, 'Why not?' These were the guys that still knew how to dream. But it wasn't easy. Now since we're on the air and successful we get about five hundred applications a week from people who want to be involved.

"So we did the first build, the Mustang lawnmower, and we're going, 'There is just no way this is going to work.' I said to Jesse, 'So, when you take off, hit it hard, make a lot of noise, and it will tear up the grass. I mean, no way it's gonna actually cut. But at least it will look great.' All of a sudden I look, and this car takes off and it hits 30, 40, 50, 60, 70 miles an hour, and, oh my God, it's cutting grass. That was one of those great defining moments in my life. We all looked at each other and got chills. It worked."

Beers comes by his garage pedigree legitimately. His father, George Beers, worked as a service manager for Ford and Chevy for 45 years. "The garage has always been a major part of my life," he says. "The smell of motor oil and metal—I love that. It's almost primal. Not to be sexist, but the garage was a place where things were handed down from father to son, or grandfather to grandson. My grandpa used to go out there to chew tobacco and putter on his Chevy. I'd watch my dad go out there with the other men in the family and laugh and tell jokes and change a spark plug or an oil filter. Now, I hear that a lot of fathers are sitting down with their sons to watch Monster Garage. My Dad calls me after every show. He's amazed by the magnitudes of the builds. He says stuff like, 'I'll be a son-of-a-gun, how do you do that?' It's cool. It's like, you know, you want to please and amaze your Dad."

What does it take to deliver this sort of demented mechanical ingenuity to an ever-increasing number of viewers who can't wait for their weekly Monster Garage fix? "I think," Beers says, "you have to have the mechanical knowledge of a 55-year-old man, the passion of a 30-year-old man, and the dreams of a 13-year-old boy. That's how it works. That's what makes Jesse brilliant too. He has all of those things, and a great sense of humor and a gift for storytelling. We, all of us, really get excited about all this—like we are still kids. Because that's what's cool about it." ◉

TRANSFORMED DREAMS

THEY FLOAT, THEY FLY, OR AT LEAST THEY TRY

Long before the invention of the automobile, people were fascinated by the idea of vehicles that not only could drive on land but also could float on the water or fly through the air. The multitasking transformed vehicles displayed on Monster Garage are but the latest in a long tradition.

In 1805 an American inventor named Oliver Evans produced a dredging vehicle he called the "Amphibious Digger." It weighed 20 tons, was able to function on land or water, and reputedly had a top speed of 4 miles per hour. Evans wasn't the only American to give the idea a shot. In 1833 the amphibious tricycle surfaced; in 1884 it was something called the "Cycle Raft," followed—with equal lack of success—by a 1905 tricycle shaped like a canoe, which was propelled by hinged paddles and converted into an ice boat in winter. Then came the Hydro-Motorcycle, Hydro Car, Hydromotor, and more.

Men of equal imagination were working toward the same goal in other parts of the world, France in particular, where in 1905 Fournier successfully combined a boat hull and an automobile chassis. Coachbuilder Jean-Henri Labourdette became famous for the skiff-style wooden coachwork of his cars, which were designed and constructed as if they were small boats. Although Labourdette's creations were never intended to go into the water, in appearance the vehicles were handsome boat-car hybrids.

Germany's Hans Tipple, who began building amphibious vehicles in 1932, invented the only successfully mass-produced and mass-marketed multipurpose vehicle, the "Amphicar." Approximately 4,500 Amphicars were manufactured between 1960 and 1967 and about half still exist. The Amphicar wasn't much of a boat (or much of a car either), but it did work. A pair of propellers mounted below the rear bumper supplied aquatic propulsion, while steering was accomplished exactly as it is on land, via the front wheels. Power was transmitted from the 43.5-horsepower Triumph Herald engine via two transmissions (one if by land and two if by sea, no doubt). There was also an electric bilge pump, just in case. President Lyndon Johnson owned one, and a

In 1805 an American inventor named Oliver Evans produced a dredging vehicle he called the "Amphibious Digger." It weighed 20 tons and functioned on land or water.

number of prominent celebrities, including Ted Danson and Dan Aykroyd, have followed suit.

In the summer of 1965, in true mad dogs and Englishmen style, two intrepid seafarers crossed the English Channel in an Amphicar. One, a Captain Bailey, reported that, "It was found better to motor up the wave with the accelerator full down, and when the top of the wave was reached to slacken off and gently motor down the other side." Indeed.

Hugh Gordon, who bought up what remained of the Amphicar inventory in 1980 and remains a major source for parts and for completely rebuilt cars, takes a more cautious tone: "You never get used to the feeling when you drive down the boat ramp and the water rolls over the windshield and you are convinced you are going to sink."

In fact, there has been but one truly successful amphibious vehicle manufactured for use by the general public rather than by the military: the Conestoga wagon.

If driving into the briny deep doesn't get the blood coursing through your veins, how about a trip into the wild blue yonder? Just as floating cars predated the invention of the automobile, so too did the flying car arrive well in advance of the Wright brothers. In 1808 Sir George Cayley designed and built a device he called the "Coachman Carrier."

The Carrier, basically a glider with a removable road carriage mounted underneath, did manage to become airborne during tests in Yorkshire, England. But it should go without saying that true flying cars did not come into being until after the invention of the automobile. Since then, there have been more than 75 patents for flying automobiles registered in the United States.

Flying automobiles have come, and gone, under many guises. There have been Air-Cars, Aero-Automobiles, Autoplanes, Sky Cars, Arrowbiles, ConvAIRCARS, Airphibians, Roadplanes, Travelplanes, Plane-Mobiles, Aerocars, Airmobiles, Aviocars, Sky Rovers, and, of course, the flying DeLorean from the movie *Back to the Future*.

The most successful in terms of road- and air-

HAPPY MOTORING, TOO, IN YOUR **Amphicar**

NJ 9087 J

WELCOME ABOARD! **Amphicar**

worthiness were Moulton B. Taylor's Aerocar and Robert E. Fulton, Jr.'s Airphibian. Powered by a 4-cylinder Lycoming aircraft engine, the Aerocar was certified by the Civil Aviation Administration in 1956. Over the next ten years, seven were built, driven, and flown successfully. But the company failed due to a lack of interest from corporate investors with sufficient money to make the venture fly.

Fulton's Airphibian, which now reposes in the Smithsonian Institution, also was victim to the timidity, or perhaps the common sense, of potential investors. The good news for those of you who can't wait to get your hands on a flying flivver comes from Fulton's three sons who, it is said, will produce new Airphibians on a special-order basis for about $500,000 apiece. Singer Jimmy Buffett is rumored to be interested, and you'd have to admit that there couldn't be a much cooler way to arrive in Margaritaville.

Last, but in terms of sheer bravado not least, are the "triphibians." Like Hollywood's "All Talking, All Singing, All Dancing" films of the early sound era, the triphibian does it all: land, sea, and air. A small number of these all-purpose vehicles have been manufactured, including the Triphibian Aeromarine.

One of the most interesting multipurpose vehicles of recent decades has to be the "Heli-Home," a sort of mobile hunting cabin. Introduced in 1977 by the Itasca Division of Winnebago Industries, it was manufactured by Orlando Helicopter Airways out of war-surplus Sikorsky helicopters and Winnebago motor homes. This eight-passenger camper flew at 100 miles per hour with a range of 350 miles, and also functioned on land and in water.

Will the success of the Monster Garage VW Swamp Buggy give rise to a host of Johnny-come-lately land-and-sea imitators? Will the Monster Garage Geo Tracker Hot Air Balloon inspire a new wave of land-and-air vehicles? As Jerry Schell, the hot air balloon expert who appeared on that episode of Monster Garage, says: "I don't think you could sell this idea to anybody." ◉

OFF-ROAD VEHICLES

VW BEETLE SWAMP BUGGY

FORD BRONCO ROCK CLIMBER

MAZDA RX7 SAND RAIL

CHEVY CORVETTE MUD BOGGER

The Amphibious Slug Bug

SWAMP BEETLE

VW BEETLE SWAMP BUGGY

"*I've seen* Deliverance."

JESSE JAMES

THE MISSION:
TURN A VW BEETLE
INTO A WORKING SWAMP BOAT

TEAM

JESSE JAMES

RICKY HSU
Car designer
GARDENA, CALIFORNIA

BRIAN JENDRO
Car customizer
TEMECULA, CALIFORNIA

JOHN KRAWCZYK
Welder and sculptor
MALIBU, CALIFORNIA

TOM PREWITT
Custom motorcycle painter
BREA, CALIFORNIA

J.D. STREETT
Special-effects supervisor
SHADOW HILLS, CALIFORNIA

CHRISTY SUMNER
Special-effects technician
LOS ANGELES, CALIFORNIA

RONNIE THIBODAUX
Boat designer and builder
CENTERVILLE, LOUISIANA

JOHN URIBE
Auto-mechanics instructor
RESEDA, CALIFORNIA

SPECS

VEHICLE
2000 Volkswagen Beetle

ENGINE
Stock VW 4-cylinder, 2-liter

TRANSMISSION
Stock automatic

**SUSPENSION-
BRAKES-STEERING**
Stock VW

PAINT
By House of Kolor. Clear coat over
three different orange pearl base
coats, one hot-pink pearl base coat,
and two coats of gold-ice pearl.

WHEELS
Stock

MONSTER SPECS
Aircraft propeller and rudders;
liquid closed-cell foam.

THE BUILD

PLAN B

CUSTOM
AUTO B

Swamp boats operate with equal dexterity on land and in the water. Well, the land part will be easy; will the water part be too? One of the two major tasks facing the build team is the installation of an airboat engine, in this case a brand new, chrome-plated, 110-horsepower, air-cooled VW engine driving a small aircraft propeller. And the whole works will have to slide in and out of a trunk that is only sixty inches deep.

The fourteen-inch carbon-fiber propeller blades deliver 1,500 pounds of thrust. To make room for these, and the rudders, the rear seat and most of the trunk panels are discarded. To increase the depth of the opening, the build team cuts into the fenders and body, then welds these pieces to the door. Sounds simple enough until you realize that the VW has unibody construction.

The second major hurdle is flotation. To float the buggy, pontoons are fabricated to fit between the fenders, then filled with AB foam for flotation. A large section of $1/8$-inch sheet aluminum seals off the bottom. Every hole, no matter how small, has to be filled in with fast-acting sealant. Rhino Lining, used to weatherproof truck beds, is lavishly applied. The exhaust pipes are another potential water entry point, because they end just under the rear bumper. The problem is solved with custom motorcycle pipes tall enough to stay above water.

Using a power hammer, Jesse fabricates a curved prow for the buggy. John Krawczyk uses a TIG (Tungsten Inert Gas) welder to attach the rudders, which fit inside the body with the door closed. A hydraulic ram is installed to push the engine out of the car into the airstream, and a fuel tank for the rear engine is placed behind the passenger seat.

Finally, at the last possible minute on the last day of the build, the crew takes the completed swamp buggy to the Long Beach Marina for a test *schwimm,* and, like Ivory Soap, it floats.

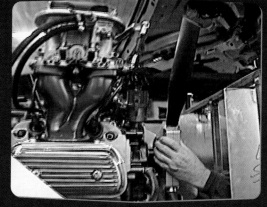

"The thing that gets you and makes you enjoy the airboat is the noise factor. I like the noise."

RONNIE
THIBODAUX

THE CHALLENGE

What got me started with airboats was about twenty-eight years ago when I first rode in one and, just like anybody else, fell in love with it. Then my buddy let me drive his boat and it was just an unbelievable experience. From that point on I had to have one. Bought me one, put it together, rode it, sold it, and just kept going on and on. Now here I am all these years later and still doing the same thing, manufacturing what I love.

"Nothing can give you the thrill that an airboat ride can. Outboards can't go where they can, mud boats can't follow. It's just a wonderful piece of equipment, and I feel fortunate that I'm able to do what I do best: build airboats.

RONNIE THIBODAUX

J esse and the rest of the Monster Garage crew travel all the way to Ronnie Thibodaux's hometown of Centerville, Louisiana, to take on Ronnie's son Neil and his 400-horsepower, big-block Chevy-engine swamp boat. It is a close race, but the power and speed of the big airboat can't make up for the time Neil loses unloading and launching it. Jesse, of course, just drives on in.

JESSE'S FINAL THOUGHTS
"That one was pretty tough—tough to make it float and still keep it semi-stock-looking, without totally making it like a boat."

" I'm used to being the only woman, you know, being drowned in testosterone. I just go home, shower it off, put on a nice floral and some flip-flops, and make dinner."

CHRISTY SUMNER

How to make a molehill out of a mountain

ROCK CRAWLER

FORD BRONCO ROCK CLIMBER

"*Rock crawler? I don't even know what it is for sure, but I'm sure I can make it.*"

JESSE JAMES

THE MISSION: TURN A THOROUGHBRED BRONCO INTO A SURE-FOOTED MOUNTAIN GOAT

TEAM

JESSE JAMES

MIKE ALLEN
Magazine editor
NEW YORK, NEW YORK

MIKE DUNCAN
4X4 specialist
BURBANK, CALIFORNIA

**BRANDON
"THE KNIFE" GILLEN**
Champion rock crawler
SANDY, UTAH

RYAN "LINDY" LINDBERG
Ford Bronco expert
LOS ANGELES, CALIFORNIA

ANDY MCCLOSKY
Attorney
SAN DIEGO, CALIFORNIA

STEVE RUMORE
Rock crawler driver and engineer
BAYFIELD, CALIFORNIA

SEAN SMITH
Artist and hot rod builder
OAK HILLS, CALIFORNIA

SPECS

VEHICLE
1968 Ford Bronco

ENGINE
Stock Ford 302, Edelbrock Pro Flow
fuel injection system, Mac exhaust
headers

TRANSMISSION
Stock C-4 automatic

SUSPENSION-
BRAKES-STEERING
Front: King coil-over shocks,
Monster Garage custom three-link;
Rear: King coil-over shocks,
Monster Garage inverted four-link;
Dynatrac disc brakes. Avalanche
Engineering full hydraulic front
and rear steering.

PAINT
Teal LINE-X polyurethane bed liner

WHEELS
Hutchinson military-style bead locks
supplied by USA6x6.com

MONSTER SPECS
Hydraulic rams for four-wheel
independent steering control;
Dynatrac Pro Rock 60 axles;
Fuel Safe fuel cell; Advanced
Adaptors Atlas transfer case;
Sparco racing seats.

THE BUILD

" *Maybe Jesse will flip it over— roll it, crash it, thrash it. Yeah, it's all good.* "

MIKE DUNCAN

The typical Day One vehicle gutting is taken to the extreme with the Bronco. In addition to the usual assault on the vehicle's interior and assorted body parts, the team removes the entire front end, rear end, drive shaft, and just about everything else. By the time the crew finishes, there is nothing left but part of the frame, the tranny, two doors, a cracked windshield, and an engine that has seen better days. Upon closer inspection it is found to be uselesss—or, as Mike Allen puts it, "Too bad it's not a boat. We'd have an anchor."

The next day sees the fabrication of a complete roll cage. Lindy brings a Mandrell bender from his shop to bend the steel tubes. Giant B.F. Goodrich Crawler TA tires arrive and are mounted on wheels with military-style bead locks originally developed for the Hummer. This will allow super-low air pressure to increase the size of the tire footprint for maximum traction.

As more parts arrive the intensity of the build increases. Time is running out and still the new engine has not materialized. The fuel cell is installed, rear axles are put into place, brackets are made for the shock and spring mountings, control arms are fabricated for the coil-over suspension, the bodywork is reconfigured to accommodate the oversize tires, and a half-top is installed to keep the Bronco looking as close to stock as possible. The engine finally arrives, is mated to the tranny and the transfer case, and, after some last-minute problem solving, is placed into the car.

At the end of Day Five the crew leaves knowing that Day Six will be a killer. They will have to mount the radiator, grille, front and rear fenders, steering rams, and rear steer valve, finish the hood, fire the motor and break in the cam, bleed all the hydraulics and the brakes, and go out and run over something large.

Day Six is everything they expected and then some. With most of the work done, they discover that they are missing some crucial hydraulic fittings. The solution is close to hand. The crew goes into the parking lot with some tools and a flashlight and removes the parts from the Mini Cooper Snowmobile, from another episode of Monster Garage.

Finally, the Bronco roars to life and goes in search of something to climb. Since there are few large boulders in Long Beach, Jesse provides a substitute in the form of a 1979 Olds Delta 88. After a minor delay, when the team blows the motor and extinguishes the resultant fire under the watchful eyes of the LBFD, the Bronco climbs all over the Olds.

THE CHALLENGE

A rock crawler is a 4x4 that is modified or constructed to maneuver over or around large rocks. It generally has high ground clearance, a low center of gravity, and large tires. A smooth undercarriage for sliding over obstacles and a winch are a must. I drove this one and was quite impressed with its ability. I would like to have had some rocks to test it out on, but there aren't any in Long Beach.

STEVE RUMORE

Jesse and the Bronco arrive at the Mojave Desert challenge site raring to go—straight up if possible. The Bronco crawls, climbs, and claws its way over some pretty impressive terrain. Jesse, determined to put every last one of the 16,000 foot-pounds of torque to work, steps on it. After a final frame-jarring leap, the tranny springs a leak followed quickly by a wrecked suspension and dislodged drive shaft—all in all, a short-lived outing. The day in the desert ends with an impromptu birthday party for Jesse, complete with cake, candles, and a smidgen of grease.

MONSTER

Rock crawling is the world's slowest automotive sport. Rock crawler drivers are slow, too.

FACTOID

JESSE'S FINAL THOUGHTS

"I thought for doing so much work for something that goes so slow, and is geared so slow, that it wouldn't be fun. We took it and drove it right over a car in my parking lot. I was proven wrong; the fans all voted that we build that and they were right, that stuff is pretty fun. It seems like one of those things that when you're totally 'faced, it's even more fun—one of those kinds of sports."

The true tale of a failed rail
DOOM BUGGY

MAZDA RX7 SAND RAIL

"We're just going to wing it. I don't know how. I mean, come on."

JESSE JAMES

THE MISSION:
TURN A MAZDA RX7 FOUR-WHEEL ROAD CAR INTO A MONOWHEEL-PROPELLED SAND RAIL

TEAM

JESSE JAMES

LIL' JOHN BUTTERA
Hot rod designer and builder
LOS ALAMITOS, CALIFORNIA

JASON CONANT
Car builder
ELK GROVE, CALIFORNIA

MIKE FERGUSON
Sand rail builder and racer
TEMPE, ARIZONA

COLE FOSTER
Car and bike customizer
SALINAS, CALIFORNIA

ANTHONY LUERA
Graphic artist and bike builder
LONG BEACH, CALIFORNIA

JIM MCKENNA
Technology services manager
ALAMEDA, CALIFORNIA

ART OSBORNE
Designer
PASADENA, CALIFORNIA

TOM PREWITT
Custom motorcycle painter
BREA, CALIFORNIA

SPECS

VEHICLE
1990 Mazda RX7

ENGINE
Stock rotary

TRANSMISSION
Stock 5-speed manual

**SUSPENSION-
BRAKES-STEERING**
Front: stock. Rear: independent,
retrofitted with EAI air-suspension
4X4-inch hard shaft, Parker
top- and side-port air cylinders.
Brakes stock. Steering stock.

INTERIOR
Cobra Seats from Sube Sports

PAINT
By House of Kolor. Black base coat
under galaxy gray, topped with
smoke metal flake and clear coat.

WHEELS
LA wire 100-spoke gold-wire
wheels with chrome

MONSTER SPECS
Jeg's fuel cell; Nitrous Express
nitrous oxide system with
10-pound bottle; two linear
actuators; EAI 5-gallon
chrome tank.

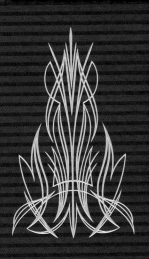

THE BUILD

66 *When I first saw the drawing, my reaction was, 'We'd better start now!* 99

JIM MCKENNA

The most important decision during the design phase is to have the rail propelled by a single rear-mounted wheel powered off the rear drive shaft. Because typical sand rails weigh in at about 1,700 pounds, the RX7 would have to shed a lot of its 3,200-pound curb weight. As always the build begins by cutting, tearing, ripping, and otherwise deconstructing the stock Mazda.

There is a lot of discussion about the various ways to fabricate the rear-wheel swing arm assembly until Jesse comes up with a workable plan. A nitrous oxide system is installed to pump up the engine horsepower in hopes that it will help to propel the heavy rail to a respectable top speed. Jesse, mindful of the appendage that his welding helmet fits on, fabricates a roll cage out of steel tubing. To give the front some additional ground clearance, an air suspension system is installed; off-road performance seats replace the stock Mazda buckets; and the heavy stock gas tank is replaced with a lightweight fuel cell.

As the final day of the build approaches, the rear-wheel swing arm assembly still is a nonstarter. On the afternoon of the last day, it all begins to come together. The swing arm assembly is welded into place, the actuators that will move the monowheel up and down are installed, and, with less than an hour to spare, the rail is ready to roll. A quick trip over to a nearby patch of sand proves that the sand rail works. But how well the vehicle will perform over open sand is not to be discovered. Before any real testing can start, the Long Beach Police Department arrives and pulls the plug. They are not amused—they probably don't watch a lot of television.

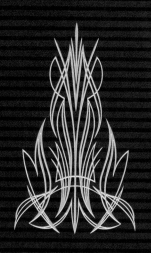

THE CHALLENGE

"What you see is what you get in the Monster Garage. It's real, it's big, and it's loaded with a bunch of tools. You get a vehicle and a drawing, and then you have to do it. The garage is kept alive by a guy named Alex Anderson. If it weren't for him we would have run out of grinding discs, steel tubing, electrical wires, electrical connections, and all the other stuff we either learned we needed or broke as we went about converting the sand rail. That guy is amazing.

"All and all, I'm proud as I can be. Our build was extremely difficult. We had pneumatics, electrics, nitrous, and a concept that does not exist in nature. We put all that together into a potent package."

JIM MCKENNA

It's a shootout under the hot Arizona sun: Jesse and the Doom Buggy against two state-of-the-art sand rails. It's a straight-up race, the kind Monster Garage loves. The flag drops and for the first hundred yards or so it's a race. But it's soon clear that the Doom Buggy is indeed doomed. It finishes third out of three, or, more aptly put in light of what lay in store for it: dead last.

Jesse's solution for what to do with the failed rail comes in the form of a Dillon Minigun. The fastest firing gun in the world, it fires 30-caliber shells at 3,000 rounds per minute. The gun loaded with tracer rounds, Jesse pulls the trigger and, in a scene reminiscent of *Apocalypse Now*, reduces the Doom Buggy to a ventilated, smoldering hulk. His fury spent, he approaches the wreckage and rips off a small piece of metal. "I saved a piece of the hearse," he said. "I'm going to save a piece of this."

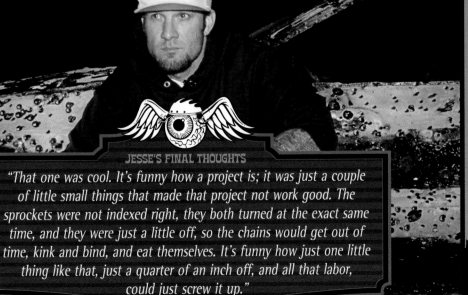

JESSE'S FINAL THOUGHTS

"That one was cool. It's funny how a project is; it was just a couple of little small things that made that project not work good. The sprockets were not indexed right, they both turned at the exact same time, and they were just a little off, so the chains would get out of time, kink and bind, and eat themselves. It's funny how just one little thing like that, just a quarter of an inch off, and all that labor, could just screw it up."

MONSTER

The world record for crossing the Sahara by camel took eleven months and killed eight camels. In the making of this Monster Garage episode, not a single camel was harmed.

FACTOID

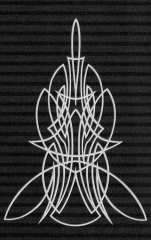

MUD BOGGER

CHEVY CORVETTE MUD BOGGER

THE MISSION: TAKE AMERICA'S FAVORITE SPORTS CAR AND MAKE IT INTO A MUD-BOGGING, DIRT-SLOGGING MONSTER

"Big motor. Big tires. Big foot."

JESSE JAMES

TEAM

JESSE JAMES

JOHN BEST
Corvette guru
BREA, CALIFORNIA

DAVE "GNARLY" COLLIER
Electrical contractor and
off-road race car fabricator
SAN MARCOS, CALIFORNIA

CHUCK COURTY, JR.
MRO mud-racing champion
PITTSBURGH, PENNSYLVANIA

DICK GULDSTRAND
Famed Corvette racer from
the 1960s. Class winner at
Le Mans, Daytona, and Sebring
BURBANK, CALIFORNIA

BOBBY MCCURDY
Mechanical workhorse
LAS VEGAS, NEVADA

MIKE STAPLETON
Off-road racing expert
BELLFLOWER, CALIFORNIA

DON VIERSTRA
Automotive artist
BUENA PARK, CALIFORNIA

SPECS

VEHICLE
1973 Chevrolet Corvette Sting Ray

ENGINE
Stock Chevy 454 Big Block

TRANSMISSION
400 Turbo

SUSPENSION-BRAKES-STEERING
Front: Racing air shocks from
King Shocks, custom-fabricated
linkage. Rear: Racing air shocks
from King Shocks, custom-fabricated
4-link with panhard
bar. No rear brakes; stock Toyota
fronts. Corvette steering box
turned 90 degrees to link up
with Toyota front end.

PAINT
By House of Kolor. White sealer,
blend created with true blue pearl,
magic blue pearl, and snow
white pearl.

WHEELS
Mickey Thompson
Challenger 15X10

MONSTER SPECS
Custom front and rear drive shafts;
Jeg's 5-gallon aluminum fuel cell;
custom-fabricated roll cage; Cobra
Racing seats from Sube Sports;
Nitrous Express nitrous tank.

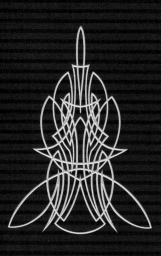

THE BUILD

" Never heard of a four-wheel-drive Corvette before. There's never been a concept of it. Now we got a concept, and we're doing it. "

JOHN BEST

When Jesse and the design team meet they quickly lay out what will be an extraordinarily difficult build: taking a stock Corvette and turning it into a four-wheel-drive bogger with off-road wheels, tires, suspension, and shocks—all in five days.

The next morning, when the build crew arrives, Jesse explains the job and gets them started with the immortal words "Gut it." By the end of the day, '73 Vette parts litter the floor of the garage. (Vintage Vette parts are worth money: The following day a guy shows up and carts the stuff away, leaving behind $800 to add to the parts budget.)

A roll cage is fabricated—just in case. The first parts to arrive are a set of Mickey Thompson wheels and tires. The large diameter of the off-road rubber means the bodywork around the wheel wells has to be cut away. This is no sooner done than the new rear and front axles arrive. The front is in such bad shape it can't be salvaged, and this means time lost while a better one is found and delivered.

A workable unit arrives the next day. Jesse lays out a stock car–style twin-link front suspension, which the build team immediately sets to work building. The biggest problem is converting the Vette from two- to four-wheel drive. The crew accomplishes this by using a chain-drive system in which twin shafts transmit power from the rear to the front axle.

The stock 190-horsepower engine will have to be boosted to 600 horsepower to keep the Vette from sinking into the mud it goes bogging through. A new cam, carburetor, and nitrous-injection system, along with special exhaust headers designed and fabricated by Jesse, do the trick, exceeding the target figure by a good 15 horses. There is one minor glitch in the process: Jesse welds on the flanges for the headers upside down and has to go back to his workbench and do them over.

On the final build day, the team fires up the motor and Jesse takes "Slingray" for a spin. (A lot of spins, actually.) Suitable mud is found in a drainage area under a nearby freeway. The monster mudder passes its initial test with flying, uh, mud.

THE CHALLENGE

It's off to the desert, where a collection of large, mean-looking off-road behemoths await the arrival of the tiny Slingray. The motors rev, the flag drops, and Jesse blasts onto the course going so fast he seems to be skimming over the surface like some mad mechanical water beetle. Does he win? He swamps 'em.

JESSE'S FINAL THOUGHTS

"That one was cool, except I blew the motor up at the end of the test. But it ran and was over 600 horsepower."

MONSTER

There are roughly 273 million acres of muddy wetlands in the U.S. It would take 130 billion Corvettes parked side by side to cover all that mud.

FACTOID

meet jesse james

"A little bit of that," Jesse James says of the tremendous media and fan attention he receives, "goes a long way." Although he certainly appreciates the popularity of Monster Garage, he is not a man who craves fame and glory. Instead, he is most at home in the world when he's working in a garage—Monster or otherwise. "All the fan stuff, I just try to keep my head out of it. Metalworking," he says, "is where my soul is."

"The more everybody tells me how great I am," he continues, "the more it makes me want to be by myself working instead of trying to live up to everybody's expectations. Just work, that's my idea. Just keep my head low and out of the bull. Keep tools in my hands. Stay away from all the hype."

The bona fide star of a hit TV series, Jesse may well become the first blue-collar television hero who actually works with his hands for a living. He's not an actor, a singer, or an entertainer. He's definitely not a talking head. He's a welder and a fabricator, one who makes awesome machines that look great, work the way they should, and go fast.

Monster Garage is a series that embraces, even glorifies, working-class values, but it combines them with the allure of the outlaw. "Outlaw" not in the negative sense but in the mythic sense, the sort most associated with

the Old West, or Hollywood's version anyway. In fact, if the names of legendary Western directors Sam Peckinpah or Sergio Leone turned up in the show's credits, they would not seem out of place.

Each episode features a band of men (mostly) who are skilled in the use of tools that appear to most people as dangerous as the six-gun of frontier times. The group is given a seemingly impossible goal that must be met in an unbelievably short amount of time. Who gives them the assignment? Who is their leader? None other than Jesse James.

As a boy in Long Beach, Jesse was your typical kid who liked to tinker with things mechanical. His father worked next door to a motorcycle-parts supplier, and Jesse began hanging around the place almost as soon as he could walk. At nine, he began customizing bikes—that's bike as in Schwinn, not Harley.

Eventually, as an adult, he turned his attention to bikes with motors; along the way, he honed his craft by working for some of the best-known metalworkers and fabricators in the business, including Boyd Coddington and Fay Butler. Jesse's reputation as a motorcycle builder is what first drew the attention of producer Thom Beers (see page 32), who worked with Jesse on the *Motorcycle Mania* television specials.

Before filming for the first season of Monster Garage began, Jesse and Thom met a number of times to talk over the kinds of vehicles they would build and to hammer out the details of what would happen during a typical episode. "I wanted to focus," Jesse relates, "on people making something out of nothing. People dig that." Although the wacky and wild finished vehicles were always part of the mix, Jesse insisted that the show also focus on the hard work and expert skills that each build would require. Thom, himself an admirer of the craftsmanship that prevails in a top-notch garage, was happy to oblige.

The first episode, Mustang Lawnmower (see page 144), ends with a fully functional, good-looking, 70-miles-per-hour grass-cutting machine. But it wasn't, Jesse admits, the smoothest episode to shoot. "I got all my friends on the build," he recalls, "and by Wednesday they all had quit. If you watch that one, I'm alone there at the end."

Now that the show receives hundreds of applications per week from designers and builders, the crews are usually first-rate. Just as he has for himself, Jesse has high standards for the men and women who work with him on Monster Garage. Good crew members, Jesse says, are the ones "who work with their hands and not with their mouth. Some of the best workers on the show aren't the most vocal. They just let their work speak for itself." He goes on to say, "It doesn't work out too well if there's someone who's hamming it up for the cameras, someone who's focused on being on TV and on how big of a star they're going to be."

Even if, once in a while, "I have to be a babysitter, like on the hearse episode [see Grim Ripper, page 168], when they were fighting over who'd get to be the welder," overall Jesse is more than impressed with the skill and dedication of the guest builders. In fact, he

GOOD CREW MEMBERS, JESSE SAYS, ARE THE ONES "WHO WORK WITH THEIR HANDS AND NOT WITH THEIR MOUTH. SOME OF THE BEST WORKERS ON THE SHOW AREN'T THE MOST VOCAL. THEY JUST LET THEIR WORK SPEAK FOR ITSELF."

says that one of the great strengths of Monster Garage is that "it shows teamwork, and highly skilled people at their best."

As a build gets under way, Jesse often takes on some of the "dirtiest jobs, and the ones with the most burns. I'll be underneath the car, for example, cutting stuff out of it." Such behind-the-scenes—or under-the-scenes—work "lets the crew know I'm not just coasting."

Once completed, some builds yield up vehicles that Jesse thinks are, well, OK, and others that he really likes. Jesse is ready with the adjectives when it comes to describing a finished vehicle that earns his approval: "It has to be wild, fun, and exhilarating—and fast and fiery. I like it when it takes skill to test it." A lack of motion is less than ideal; "standing there and chipping wood," Jesse says of the Wood Chipper episode (see page 94), "is pretty lame." If the vehicle goes fast—does exactly the opposite of "standing there," in other words—like the Snowmobile (page 14), the Wheelie Ambulance (page 128), or the Stock-Car Street Sweeper (page 156), it gets a place on Jesse's A-list. ◉

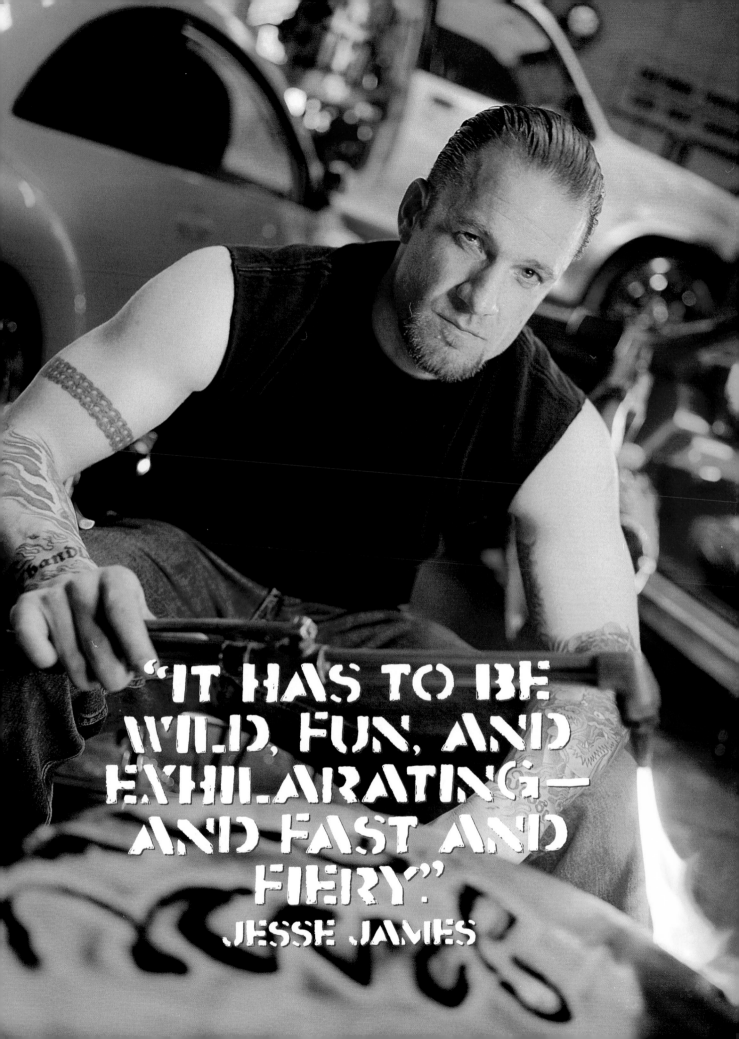

"IT HAS TO BE WILD, FUN, AND EXHILARATING— AND FAST AND FIERY."
JESSE JAMES

Hollywood Comes to Monster Garage

Jesse James and The Terminator—
it's a combination made, if not in heaven,
certainly in the next best place: Hollywood.
For the final show of what had proved to
be a stupendously successful (sounds like
Hollywood already) first season, the Monster
Garage team would take two of the main
props from the upcoming *Terminator 3*
movie, a Toyota Tundra Pickup and a Triumph
Bonneville motorcycle, and combine them
to produce a monster vehicle worthy of both
Jesse James and Arnold Schwarzenegger.

DAY ONE

The design team for this formidable task,
in addition to Jesse, is comprised of
famed "low-brow" auto artist The Pizz,
Terminator 3 production designer Jeff
Mann, and Schwarzenegger's stunt
double, Monte Perlin. The original
concept was to relocate the engine to the
truck bed and mount the motorcycle inside the empty
engine bay where it would be shot, blasted, or
somehow catapulted out while the truck was speeding
down the road. The Pizz, for one, thought that would
be neat. "If it was up to me," he says, "we would have
blown the car off and a monster claw would have come
out and dropped the bike on the ground, and there
would be flames and stuff, but we're not doing a
cartoon. It's still pretty exciting; we really are
stretching the envelope. It's not something that's going
to sit and do nothing. It has to move. It has to launch
another vehicle. So to be able to pull that off in five

days is going to be something else."

It is finally decided that the motorcycle will be placed in the passenger area and be launched out of the side of the truck by means of some sort of hydraulic-lift-gate apparatus. Jeff Mann accepts the need for the side-launch platform. "My initial perception of what we could do with this particular gag," Mann relates, "was a little more kind of mechanized than where we finally arrived. A gag is basically an effect, stunt, or something that you create because you can't go and buy it. It's something like, we really need the snake's belly to grow to the size of a basketball, and you know you're not going to find that without making it yourself, so that becomes the snake gag. It's the stick-in-the-eye gag—whatever. This is the bike-launching-from-the-side-of-the-truck gag. If it works, it will be kind of sophisticated and cool."

Monte Perlin, not unreasonably hoping to live long enough to do *Terminator 4*, is happy that the team was rethinking the plan. "I have broken my ankle, crushed my ankle, broken my back, wrists, ribs, and arm, got knocked out a few times—that's the name of the game. Everything is a risk. Anything can go wrong. Something could get caught and you could tumble under. The danger factor is there. But with the design of these guys, I'm confident that they know what they're doing. We'll get this thing dialed in at a slow speed and then work up to where we can go right at it."

Jesse, of course, has his own take on things. "We're not stuntmen, we're fabricators. We don't build stuff for the movie industry. So if he totally eats it, they should have gone to a stunt place, not Monster Garage. But we're gonna get the bike out of the truck and close to the ground. He's gotta do the rest."

DAY TWO

With the design set, it's time for the build crew to do their thing. Jesse shows them the truck and explains what they must accomplish during the next five days and nights. "You guys," he says, "are probably wondering what's it do, what's it for, why? Basically we're doing a stunt vehicle. I'll drive it and the stunt guy will be sitting in there on the bike. The bike is going to come out of the side, we'll put it down to ground level, and he'll be able to ride off and do whatever, and then ride it back on. You've got to remember that in the movies everything is ninety percent special effects and ten percent functioning parts. But this is really going to work, be slick, and be cool."

Before being turned loose in the garage, the build team gets a talk from garage manager Alex Anderson on proper procedures, including the ordering of parts. Here's the way it works, according to Alex:

"I have to get the parts, okay? They make a shopping list that says get potatoes, and if they want red russet potatoes, then they should put red russet potatoes. Because if I come back with Idahos, and they go, 'No, we wanted russets,' I'm gonna go, 'No, that's not what you put on there.' So if you say you want fittings for an air bag—there's forty different fittings you can buy. All of them would work depending on what you're doing. I'm not out there and I don't see what they are doing all the time. Sometimes I'm on the phone, or I'm doing other stuff in the shop. The easiest way to do that is just say you want 'three 90-degree $\frac{3}{8}$ NPT tube half-inch air lines.' Then I know it's not a guess."

THE BUILD CREW

DWAINE JUNGEN, 41, TUCSON, ARIZONA
"I'm married with two children and two grandchildren. I own a company called Preferred Chassis Fabrication. It's a little company, just my wife and I. My son, who's twenty-five, and a good friend of mine had been bugging me that I needed to fill out an application for Monster Garage. I'd been watching the show and I think it's really neat that Jesse is a fabricator. Fabricators and mechanics usually don't get very much prestige in today's society. Finally, they bugged me so much that I sent an application out and the next morning at ten, I had a response. I made a resume and got a portfolio together, made an audition tape, and here I am. It all happened in less than three weeks."

SEAN GIBBS, 37, MIDDLETOWN, CALIFORNIA
"I was six years old when I went to my first drag race. I still remember it to this day: Freemont Raceway, my dad used to race his car there. At seven I got my first real bicycle, and I started tearing it apart every day. Taking it apart, putting it back together—I always had all these extra nuts and bolts lying around. So my dad would show me where they all went. He told me to stop taking it apart, but I would still do it anyway. I worked as a welder and pipefitter for fifteen years, mainly in power plants, so I did industrial welding all the time. I watched a couple of episodes of *Monster Garage,* then I saw *Motorcycle Mania,* and how Jesse uses his hands. The guy is just a master with his hands."

PAUL MOORE, 34, SEASIDE, CALIFORNIA
"I was the son of a mechanic. I was helping my dad out in the shop when I was big enough to hold a wrench. He planted the seed and my stepfather watered it. I'm in school now, trying to finish a bachelor's degree in engineering. I'll always be into cars. I like it too much. I don't know what else to do. It's amazing. I was playing around online and just applied to be on the show, and two weeks later, here I am."

ERIC ROY ORTEGA, 33, CYPRESS, CALIFORNIA
"I must have been nine or ten years old when I first got interested in cars. I was working with my brother-in-law on an old Dodge. So actually, I blame him for it. I'm a hot rod builder for California Street Rods. I do all the wiring, most of the assembly, and small fabrication, and I order parts. I was playing on the computer one day, and my buddy told me about Monster Garage. I logged on and the next thing you know the guys were calling me back. Everything started getting exciting from there."

TOM CONARD, 24, TORRANCE, CALIFORNIA
"I've been around cars since I was a little kid back in New Jersey. When I went to college, automotive technology management was my major. After I got my bachelor of science degree, I got a job with Toyota and moved to California. I'm in the alternative-fuel vehicles and equipment program. I'm just this guy who sits in a cubicle all day and writes reports. I've been watching Monster Garage since it came on. I put in an application on the website, they called me back, I did an interview, and then I got called back to come here."

The build team begins work on the first build day (Day Two): They slash and burn everything not needed for the finished vehicle. Here is how Day Two, and then the rest of the build, proceeded, in the words of the participants:

Tom: "We basically got to know one another, found out what each person's area of expertise was, and learned where things were in the shop. I had to take notes so I wouldn't plug the plasma cutter into the wrong outlet; each wall had a different amp rating and I didn't want to be the one who screwed up and blew the fuse."

Sean: "The inside of my head started to work at trying to process the whole idea of the build. I was creating a mental image of the truck with a motorcycle inside the cab. The whole time we were dismantling the truck, I was thinking about fabricating the lift mechanism. After the truck was gutted, I took some measurements for the new frame section; then, after the steel arrived, I went to work on it. We had to move the frame over eighteen inches to make room for the lift. While I was building the frame, Paul and Tom started working on the door and Dwaine and Eric on the rear suspension."

Paul: "Initially we had been informed that we were to move the engine to the rear of the truck and that the front would somehow open up to deploy the bike. Whew!

The new plan was still interesting, but much easier. I took the lead on constructing the door, which consisted of skinning the passenger door, the rear door, and about a foot of the bed. The plan was to build a framework and marry all three pieces together to make one big door, reinstalled on a hinge to open with a linear actuator—like a gull wing door exposing the entire right side of the cab. I was told Jesse was trying to track down a lift gate."

Dwaine: "After discussing what parts would be needed, I made a parts list on a donut box and gave it to Alex. Sean and I discussed the frame modification. Jesse wanted the frame removed even with the front of the rear tire, and that meant that the rear suspension also would need to be modified."

Sean: "Dwaine tore out the rear end, cut up the leaf springs, and reassembled the suspension. I looked at it and thought we were going to have problems because the rear end was supported only by the back half of the leaf springs. He and I had a powwow over it and came up with the idea of a third link welded to the top of the rear end."

Paul: "The size of the bike meant the removal of a leaf spring on the right rear of the truck. It was decided that the rear should be bagged [using hydraulically operated air-bag suspension units]. Eric was busy making bits and pieces and plumbing for the air bags, while I spent most of the day working on the door, ordering an actuator and various parts. After a long first day we stopped to contemplate various aspects of the build, then we called it quits around 8:30 at night."

DAY THREE

Sean: "Jesse had located a vendor with some possible lift ideas, so Eric and I went to the lift company to check it out. The first one they showed us was completely wrong: It looked like a small crane with a cable to lift the bike off the truck. The second was a lift that mounted under the truck. It was too long and narrow, and cost $3,000—there goes the budget. I was really starting to get stressed out when the guy said they also had a lift-gate division. So off we went. One lift gate looked good but needed to be modified to make it work. After bargaining on a price, we settled on $500."

Paul: "I was out of the loop on the lift gate. Sean and Eric made an incredible find, a lift gate in good working condition. We unloaded it, sized it up, fed some power to it—all systems go. We lucked out."

Dwaine: "I welded the panhard bar brackets for the rear suspension, installed the panhard bar, manufactured the air-bag mounting plates, welded the bottom plate to the spring bolts and the top to the frame stops, and installed the air bags."

Tom: "We had to weld the door, frame it out, then hook up the actuator. Paul did most of the door-skin work while we all helped install and make it fit properly. My job was to see that the actuator would fit while having the driver's side door closed."

Sean: "Things were going good. We cut out the floor pans and that was about it for the day. I didn't get to mount the lift like I wanted to, so I was not very happy when I left the shop that night. I made up my mind to take the lead on the lift, which was the most important part of the project."

DAY FOUR

Paul: "That was a big day. The rear suspension was finished up, bags installed and checked. Jesse was around most of the day, and it was the first opportunity we had to work with him. Prior to today we hadn't seen him much, which is probably just as well, because when he moves through the room it's a major distraction. He's like a giant magnet. People start flowing in and out of the set, cameras zero in, and it's a trip to watch. Little work gets done. We weren't sure how to approach Jesse when he did start working with us. You wonder how he'll react to you, because you know it's his show and you've seen how he can relate to a builder whose company he doesn't enjoy. His attitude was quite the opposite. He had memorized our names and was totally cool. He pulled you into the show, made you feel a part of it."

Dwaine: "The lift gate was fitted to the truck. The rear cab wall and the front of the right-bed quarter panel were removed. The lift gate was lengthened to make the 'pad' long enough for the bike."

Sean: "I was loaded for bear—don't get in my way or you'll get run over. That was my attitude. I mounted the lift, showed it to Jesse, who liked it and had some great ideas. After installing the lift in the truck, I helped to fit the door. Paul did a great job on the door. Dwaine worked on the rear suspension, adding a third link to the rear end, and Eric and Tom worked on the air bags."

One highlight of Day Four is a little surprise executive producer Thom Beers has arranged for Jesse. This is the last show of the first season, so a small celebration is definitely in order—cake, candles, and ... a Ferret?

No, not the little furry things that hide under the sofa; this Ferret is a British Army war-surplus armored personnel carrier, complete with grenade launchers and a 50-caliber machine gun. To say that Jesse is happily surprised would be an understatement. He actually has a hard time wiping the smile off his face for the photographer. Once the celebrations are over, it's back to work for the build crew.

Paul: "Sean set to work making an extension for the platform to help facilitate loading and unloading the bike. This was a necessary modification, but it posed a problem:

How do we get this hinged platform extension to fold up with the rest of the gate? We wrestled with some bad ideas for a while until Dwaine came up with the winning hand, a simple solution that only required welding some square stock at either end of the lift gate. Kudos, Dwaine."

Sean: "At the end of the day we put the bike up on the lift and gave it its first test. It worked, but the bike barely fit inside. Jesse said we would have to lower the bike to make it fit right."

DAY FIVE

Sean: "It was time to fit the door, make the linkage for the lift, wire the air bags, and lower the bike. Eric fabricated the linkage while Dwaine and Tom worked on the bags. The door fit great. It was on in a couple of hours."

Paul: "I was expecting some fit problems, hinge problems, actuator problems, you name it. I had created the door and actuator system away from the truck, as too much work was being done in that area to facilitate test-fitting anything. I was concerned with the actuator mounting point at the door. The actuator was welded to a mount on the roll cage above the driver's head and extended to meet the door. No worries, mate—the 750-pound actuator lifted the door effortlessly, and we were stoked."

Tom: "Eric and I plumbed and ran all the electronics for the air bags."

Sean: "I started working on lowering the bike. I lowered the front by loosing up the triple tees and sliding the fork tubes up. Then I lowered the back by cutting off the shock mounts and moving them to the very back of the swing arm. It lowered the bike by two inches. We tested the bike on the lift again. It worked better but I noticed the lift was flexing, so I reinforced it with twenty-five welds and it was solid after that."

Dwaine: "Paul and I started on the cab cage which was used to give support to the lift-gate frame, provide protection to the driver, and provide attachment points for the gull wing door hinge and door actuator. Eric worked on the linkage and lever assembly to operate the lift gate."

Paul: "The rest of the day was spent cleaning up details

on the build. Jesse had started making a new front bumper out of round tube. The plan was to create a small platform and grab-rail for a cameraperson. Eric and I started working on joining a little section of the bed to the door, and I think Eric also set to work on grafting back onto the truck a rear corner section of the cab that we had earlier removed. Sean was busy installing steel plate to the surface of the platform extension."

Tom: "I installed the tonneau cover and mounted it. We just kind of hung out and did little odds and ends so they had stuff to shoot on Friday."

Sean: "We were basically done on Day Four."

Dwaine: "The lift gate worked—end of day."

DAY SIX

Sean: "What a fun day. We did finish and detail most of the day. I think we had the most completed project of any build."

Dwaine: "I made permanent frame stops and extension levers for the lift extension. Sean moved the foot pegs and modified the rear brake lever on the bike. Paul and Tom made final adjustments on the door. Eric trimmed and reinstalled the rear cab wall and window frame. Tom and I wired the lights in the lift gate on separate flashers, and I made a micro switch mount on the cage to actuate off the door actuator to control the door operation and the gate lights. Jesse finished his push bumper, and the truck was ready to test."

Paul: "I made a Plexiglas rear quarter window, and I notched out a section of the new bed cover for motorcycle clearance. Sean made some nylon skids for the bottom of the platform. Eric made a Maltese cross knob for the lift-gate linkage, and a cool set of Jesse James Wheels were installed as well. It was ready to roll. Mission accomplished."

Eric: "It was fun—totally different from my regular job. Now I know why they call it Monster Garage."

Sean: "I got to drive the truck. What a blast to drive down the road with straight pipes roaring. We were going to do the test on Jesse's Honda CR250, but it wouldn't fit on the lift. I wondered what we were going to do, but then I heard this noise from a little motorcycle. It was Jesse on his five-year-old son's Honda peewee 50. It was great. We did the test and it went off without a hitch. I lowered him off the lift, he exited the lift, and he re-entered the lift. I raised him back into the truck and drove off into the sunset. What a beautiful day."

Dwaine: "Jesse did the stunt on his son's Honda and everything went great. It was a success. The truck drove down there and drove back, the air-conditioning worked, everything worked flawlessly. It's just fantastic."

Tom: "I tried to do it on my BMX bike, but it was harder than it looked. Jesse tried it on the XR50 and it was a success."

Paul: "It will be interesting to see how the stuntman will pull it off at 50 miles an hour. We reconvened at the set, collected our stuff, took a few pictures, grabbed some autographs, and headed back to our regular lives. I'll never forget that week, my fifteen minutes of fame and Monster Garage."

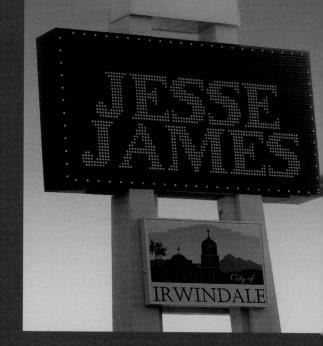

THE CHALLENGE

When the time comes for the final test, the challenge crew takes the motorcycle-truck combo to Irwindale Speedway, where stuntman Monte Perlin will get his first loo at the completed vehicle and climb aboard what will prove to be an exciting ride.

Monte: "I didn't know quite what to expect. I've bee doing stunts for over twenty years now, and I never ha done one like this. When I saw this unique modified bi hauler, I was totally surprised—couldn't wait to get in a try it out. I loved the workmanship and the hydraulics. course, like any new stunt, I pondered on the best way go about it. I got on the Triumph, entered in, and they closed it up. I tried a dry run with the truck at a standstill. It was so cool and felt good.

"We decided to shoot the rehearsal at a slow speed t see what could happen and then speed up. It all went great, so we increased the speed. Once I was out and d some wheelies and a few tricks, I rode back onto the platform and the crazy contraption tucked me back insi closed up, and with Jesse driving we proceeded to do slides and 360s. I was very impressed with the mechani the prep, and the safety of the whole thing. I loved it!"

Some final thoughts from the producer of this episo Ned Judge, and from Jesse:

Ned: "It was quite a culture shift, coming from PBS and stepping into Monster Garage. It's great fun, like taking a hit of that mustard they put in sushi. Monster Garage clears your sinuses. It's rock 'n' roll video—everything I expected, squared."

Jesse: "This one was totally easy—no real challenge, don't think, because it doesn't do anything. It's just a platform to ride on. It was no fun for me. Once you rid bike on and off about three times, then it's like, I've do that—next? Usually for the week's worth of work, I wan little more prize than that. The challenge was cool. Monte's a pretty good rider."

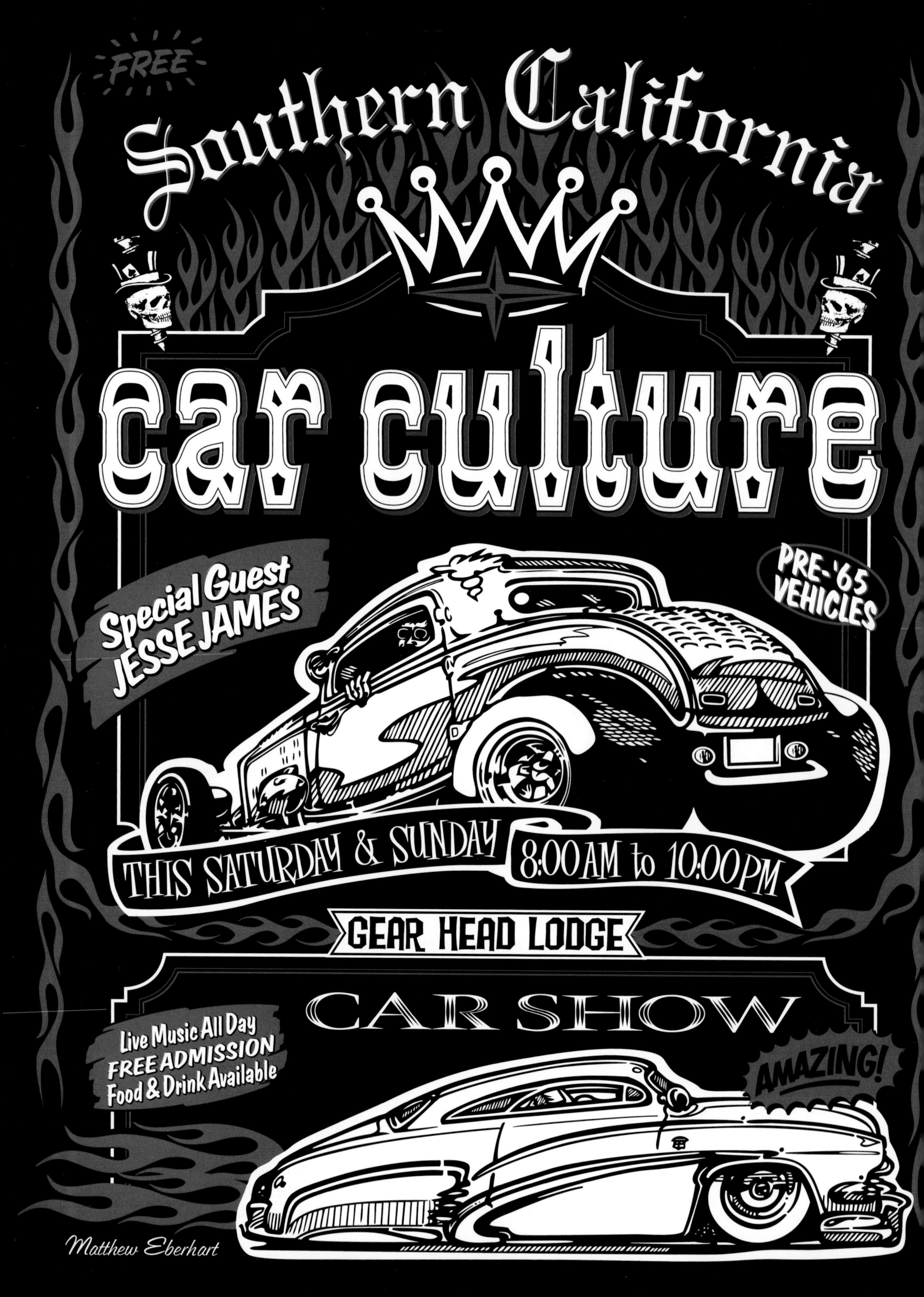
FREE
Southern California
car culture
Special Guest JESSE JAMES
PRE-'65 VEHICLES
THIS SATURDAY & SUNDAY
8:00AM to 10:00PM
GEAR HEAD LODGE
CAR SHOW
Live Music All Day
FREE ADMISSION
Food & Drink Available
AMAZING!
Matthew Eberhart

Hot Rods,
Low Riders, and California Dreaming

If you think it strange that California, with its clogged freeways and performance-draining emissions standards, is the undisputed car culture capital of America, just remember where Route 66 ends.

The urge to customize or otherwise modify your wheels has existed since the first automobiles hit the streets, and not just in Southern California. But when you riff on hot rods, it's the Beach Boys, *American Graffiti*, drive-ins, and other Californiana that fill the canyons of your mind. Jesse James and Monster Garage, both of which hail from Long Beach, are the inheritors of this Golden State tradition.

Hot rods, or hot roadsters as they were first called in the 1920s and 1930s, were the young blue-collar worker's answer to those who could afford the latest Detroit iron.

The real hot rod movement began at the end of World War II when thousands of servicemen returning to the U.S from the Pacific Theater disembarked in California. When they walked down the gangplank in San Francisco, San Diego, or Long Beach, they had their mustering-out pay, good mechanical and engineering skills courtesy of Uncle Sam, and a hankering for their own set of wheels. But wheels, as they soon found out, were in short supply.

Domestic automobile manufacturing had ceased during the war years, so the first post-war cars were made from pre-war designs. Cars were in short supply, and they were expensive. If the new-car dealerships or even the used-car lots didn't offer an affordable option, what could? The answer was junkyards. California's junkyards, and the small speed-equipment shops that were springing up everywhere, gave the returning GI the means to assemble his own car—often a two-seater that looked cool and took off like a bat: the hot rod.

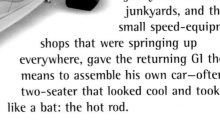

Photography: Top, Beatrice Neumann
Bottom, Dave Lindsay

So a hot rod is fast and it looks good. But a hot rod is also something else: It's a different vehicle. A hot rod is a standard Detroit automobile that has been modified and transformed, and, unlike standard mass-produced vehicles, has become a personal expression of the person who built it.

Another metalbending group with deep roots in California, and with a vibrant subculture there to this day, is the custom motorcycle builders. Their creations, at first typified by the custom choppers that burst on the scene in 1969 with the release of the film *Easy Rider,* have evolved to such an extent that some makers are no longer content to modify existing bikes (invariably Harleys) but now design and build their dream machines from the ground up.

In the early 1970s, when the hot rod craze had finally peaked in the media and street racing had mostly given way to events sanctioned by the National Hot Rod Association (NHRA), a new form of individual automotive expression began to emerge in the public consciousness: the low rider. Where the hot rodder's credo is fast and furious, the low rider's motto is low and slow.

A low rider can be either a vehicle or the person who drives the vehicle. Low rider culture, which began in the Hispanic-American enclaves of East Los Angeles, has now spread to communities of all ethnicities throughout the country. There are, for example, a growing number of African-American practitioners of "low and slow" car design and driving. (And there is even a growing low rider culture in Japan.)

What is a low rider? It's a car that has been lowered to the point where the bottom of the body hovers above, or just grazes, the street. The first low riders accomplished this by cutting down the front coil springs and taking most of the arch out of the rears. But the low rider is much more than a lowered vehicle. It is an example of craftsmanship and artistry seldom found on any other vehicles. It is also a lifestyle: a community of like-minded people, families, and fraternal clubs, who gather together to celebrate and preserve their heritage.

The low rider vehicle, and it can be anything on wheels, features lots of chrome, or gold plating, candy-color and metal-flake paints, overstuffed cloth or leather interiors, glass etchings, and murals depicting social, historic, religious, and fantasy themes. If coachbuilt cars are, as anointed by the Museum of Modern Art, "rolling sculpture," then low riders are rolling artwork. They also can hop, skip,

The low rider is much more than a lowered vehicle. It's an example of craftsmanship and artistry.

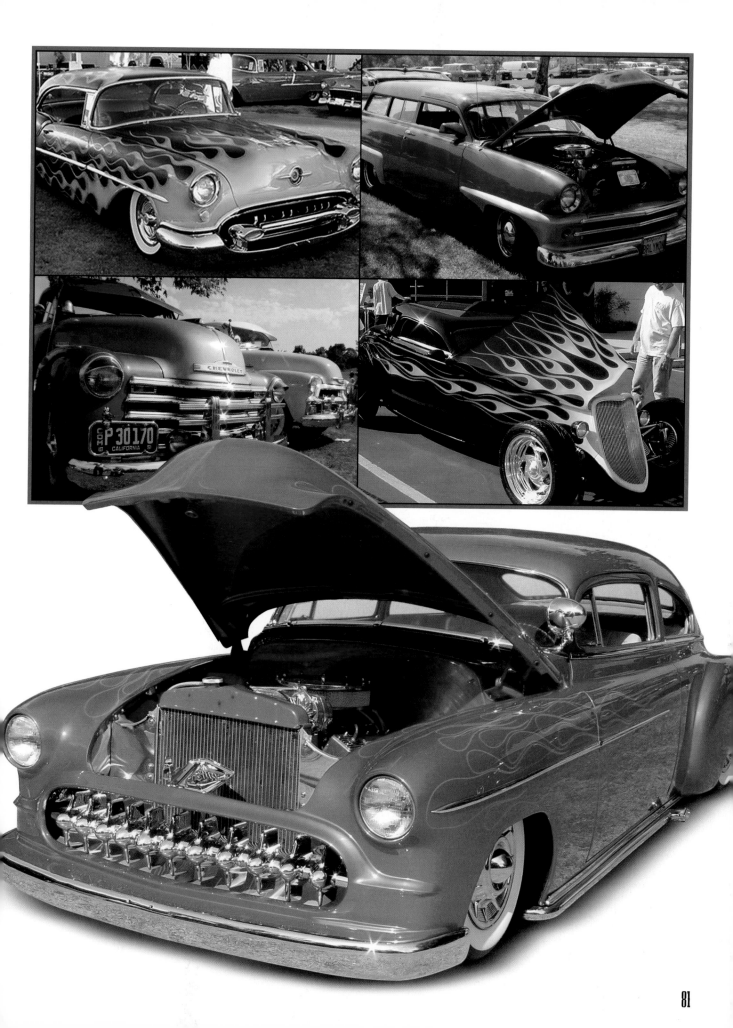

and jump. (Definitely not your grandfather's Duesenberg.) Many low rider cars are equipped with banks of batteries and hydraulic air-bag suspension systems; they are "juiced." These systems permit the driver to make his ride hop up and down, move side to side, or, if it's really radical, dance. Bed dancing competitions feature mini-trucks with hinged frames that allow the truck bed to open up, out, and all over the place. The driver has become an operator who stands to the side and directs his motorized creation via remote control.

Hot rods and low riders are perfect examples of vehicles whose transformations, while completely individualistic, are also a product of their times and cultures. Although still able to perform the functions for which they were designed, to drive to the beach on Sunday, say, they transcend their functionality and become, to use a three-letter word: art. ☺

"Customizers, like their counterparts in the contemporary art world, used the materials and images of their times to reflect and comment on the values of American society and on the speed of change. As distinct cultures, hot rodders and low riders reveal feelings of alienation and belonging, rebellion and community, movement and individuality." – NORA DONNELLY

Curator, Customized: Art Inspired by Hot Rods, Low Riders, and American Car Culture. Institute of Contemporary Art, Boston

MONSTER ART

HIGH-BROW, MIDDLE-BROW, LOW-BROW, OR NO-BROW: THERE'S AN ART TO WHAT HAPPENS ON MONSTER GARAGE.

Most of us would agree that there are hot rods, low riders, and other customized and modified vehicles that achieve the status of *objets d'art*—even if we wouldn't use such a high-falutin phrase to describe them. Are there also art objects that achieve the status of, well, vehicles? The answer appears to be yes.

Venetian artist Livio De Marchi has sculpted a number of handsome vehicles out of wood, including a Jaguar, a Mercedes, a Ferrari, and a 1,500-pound replica of a VW Beetle. Designed to float and powered by a 10-horsepower motor mounted in the rear, the aquatic Beetle churns along at five miles an hour. Another artwork is *Knife Ship 1* by famed pop art master Claes Oldenburg. Reminiscent of a Swiss Army Knife with oars, *Knife Ship 1*, too, has successfully motored on the canals of Venice. (Italy, that is, not California.)

One current artist and teacher, California-based Rubén Ortiz-Torres, is constantly exploring the relationship between high and low art, particularly as it applies to California car culture in general and, more specifically, the world of the low rider. Born in Mexico, Ortiz-Torres's work encompasses paintings, photographs, film, video, multimedia collage, and customized commercial products. You can see his work in a number of prominent institutions, including the Museum of Modern Art and the Metropolitan Museum of Art in New York.

"I think people in the United States are really aware of other cultures," Ortiz-Torres says. "Not necessarily art but, say, music or movies. Everybody goes to see the recent things and has some sort of opinion. I would say the same about car culture. People are very aware of the attention to craft and to certain concerns that would relate to art in a way that it is very hard for me to address even in an art class.

"In the art world people are still arguing about how to engage in figuration and abstraction. To my surprise, working with car painters or with low riders, it's not an issue. Cars can have figurative paintings, or they can just have paint jobs where they are purely abstract, although their creators wouldn't call them abstract. That just shows me how sophisticated their aesthetic judgment can be.

"One of the things that really fascinated me the first time I started looking at these things is the obsession with customizing the function of the car—for example, gold-plating the brakes. Nobody is going to see that. It's not just impractical, it's absurd; and yet it becomes a meaningful part."

If there is one work of Ortiz-Torres that vividly expresses in action what the artist has put into words it is *Alien Toy: (Unidentified Cruising Object),* a 1997 video installation on wheels. The installation is centered around the low rider pickup truck "Wicked Bed," which was created by multiple-world-champion bed-dancing master Salvador "Chava" Muñoz, a man Torres places in the "the avant-garde of low rider culture": "Salvador came from Jalisco [in Mexico] to California. As an outsider from the low rider community, he was able to free himself from the classicism of the Chevy Impala. He is a self-taught iconoclast. Like some sort of Doctor Frankenstein, he has given life to this aggressive, irrational machine. The future is happening and is out of control like a mutated virus. Technology has been appropriated; it can become a culture jamming in the streets."

This monster of a machine features sixteen hydraulic systems that disassemble and propel the truck in ways you wouldn't believe. It is capable of fragmenting itself into four separate sections, each

Rubén Ortiz Torres, Alien Toy, 1997. Collection Tom Patchett, Los Angeles.
Courtesy Track 16 Gallery, Santa Monica

The Pizz. *Oskorei (Wild Hunt)*

operating independently of the others, and it can send the bed of the truck into the air where it, too, divides into four separate, spinning parts. The doors pop out, the hood lifts off and twirls, and, most amazingly, the entire cab separates from the rest of the truck and drives around while the remaining parts of the truck continue to gyrate.

Alien Toy might even be viewed as the ultimate Monster Garage-style creation, one that could push the envelope of popular television programming in completely new directions. Ortiz-Torres has his own take on the program: "What I really like about Monster Garage is that it's complicated, because the issue of aesthetics is always involved. It's not just about making the thing work; it's that you have to make it cool. It has to be cool. That for me makes it more complicated aesthetically."

Producing works of "art" might be the last thing to which Jesse and the Garage gang would admit. Then again, maybe not. Jesse is the owner of a major piece of what its creator, the Pizz, calls, "low-brow art." According to Pizz:

"Jesse wanted a big painting. I was looking around for a theme and I found this old Viking legend of Oskorei, which means wild ride or wild hunt. The legend has it that at a certain time of the year, around harvest time like our Halloween, the heavens would open up and the heroes in Valhalla would come out of the sky and rampage through the countryside. What

could be more biker than that? It's kind of this updated legend: there's a skeleton biker dude on a big chopper, and he's going through a bombed-out cityscape of rubble, crashed trucks, and cars."

The Pizz is part of an unaffiliated group of "low-brow" artists whose work is closely identified with California's car culture: Ed "Big Daddy" Roth (with whom the Pizz worked), Von Dutch, Coop, Jimmy C, Von Franco, and Robert Williams. Williams has his own take on the Pizz:

"If you were to force Pizz to paint Currier and Ives landscapes or pictures of sweet little puppies, you would defile Pizz. He works for his will, not for his wallet. Five hundred years ago he would have either been in the court of kings or on the gallows."

When Jesse asked Pizz to join the design team for a Monster Garage build, he didn't have to think twice about it. "I think," says the Pizz, "Monster Garage is pretty cool, because you're taking one of the defining products of American culture—the automobile, something that people buy as a status symbol to define who they want to be and who they think they are—and twisting it into something unimaginable, something that goes. Western culture is all about going. We as Americans have really perfected that to an art form where our cars, bikes, our whole lifestyle are about velocity and going."

Okay, let's go.... ⚙

Utility Vehicles

CHEVY
STEP VAN
DELIVERY
TRUCK

PT
CRUISER
WOOD
CHIPPER

FORD
F-150
PICKUP
NUT
SHAKER

HOT
DOG
CART
DRAGSTER

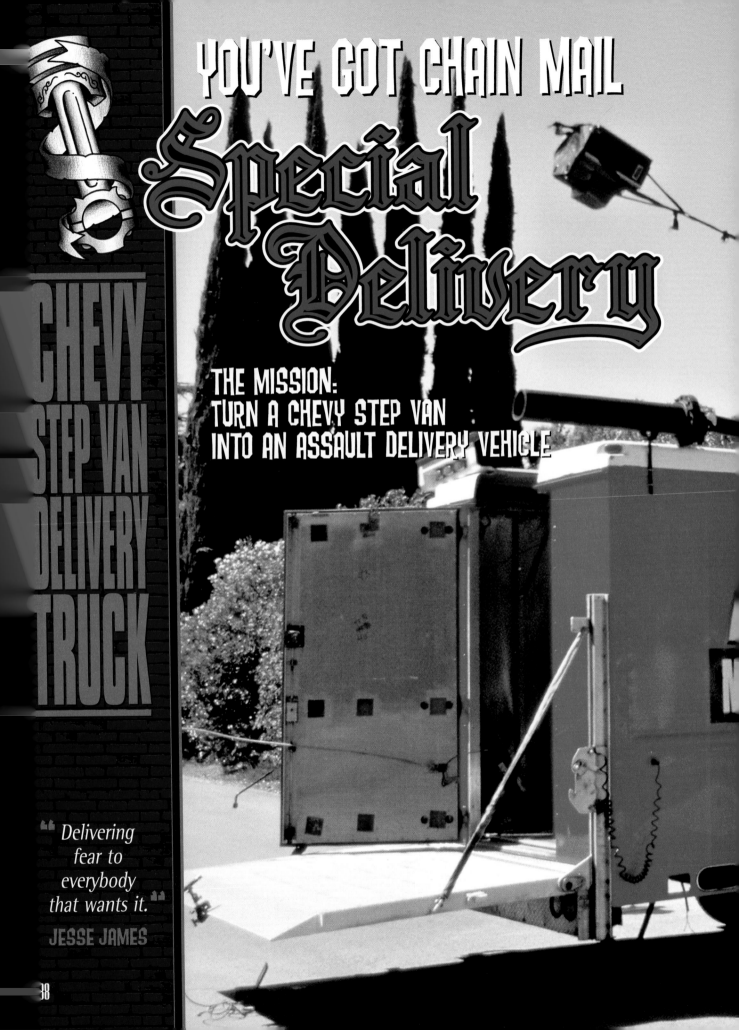

YOU'VE GOT CHAIN MAIL
Special Delivery

THE MISSION:
TURN A CHEVY STEP VAN
INTO AN ASSAULT DELIVERY VEHICLE

CHEVY STEP VAN DELIVERY TRUCK

"Delivering fear to everybody that wants it."

JESSE JAMES

Team

JESSE JAMES

PAUL CAMPBELL
Plastic-surgery nurse
SANTA MONICA, CALIFORNIA

JIM FARLEY
Truck mechanic and hot rodder
RENO, NEVADA

DAIS NAGAO
Artist and motorcycle designer
PASADENA, CALIFORNIA

TOM PREWITT
Custom motorcycle painter
BREA, CALIFORNIA

DAVID NORRIS
Inflatable-signage expert
PHOENIXVILLE, PENNSYLVANIA

RON TOMS
Medieval weaponry expert
LOS ANGELES, CALIFORNIA

J'ME WHITLOCK
Fabricator, welder, and artisan
COSTA MESA, CALIFORNIA

Specs

VEHICLE
1998 Chevy P-1000 Step Van;
Body by Grumman Olson Industries

ENGINE
Stock 205-horsepower diesel

TRANSMISSION
Allison Automatic

SUSPENSION-
BRAKES-STEERING
Stock

PAINT
By House of Kolor. Six coats
blue-blood red,
six coats clear sealer.

WHEELS
Stock

MONSTER SPECS
Dual four-chamber Gatling
gun-style air cannons with a
firing pressure of 150 to 350
pounds per square inch that can
fire newspapers over 200 feet;
single six-inch-barrel air cannon
with a firing pressure of 150 to
350 pounds per square inch that
can fire a small package 50 to
75 feet; a trebuchet that exerts
1,800 pounds of force and is
capable of hurling a 50-pound
object 500 to 600 feet; a ballista
that exerts 1,200 pounds of force
and can hurl a 20-pound object
50 to 75 feet.

The Build

" Sometimes it's fun just to go out and shoot bowling balls a few hundred feet. "

RON TOMS

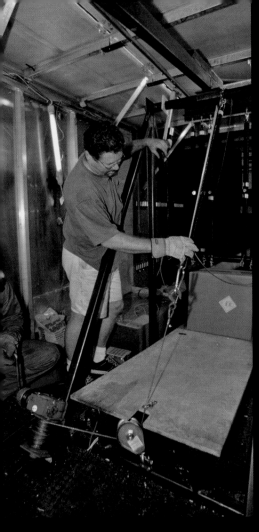

The biggest challenge faced by this team is the tight space into which they have to fit all of the complex machinery necessary to complete the challenge. The van interior includes tool display racks, a toolbox area and toolbox restraint system, display shelving, an eight-drawer desk, sliding display drawers, auxiliary battery, pegboard, insulation, flooring, two air-tool displays, fire extinguisher, meter test panel, fourteen lights, and an alarm system. Well, we know what happened to all of that, right? (Except the alarm—but please don't ask.)

Once the truck is gutted, work begins on the various artillery components. The trebuchet frame is fabricated, and springs to provide the hurling power along with a winch to cock it are purchased and connected. Pelican hooks from a maritime supply shop will become the triggers to release the trebuchet. While the roof of the truck is cut open, a support beam is installed and hinges are put into place. The ballista and its eight-foot-long arms are fabricated. Compressed air tanks await the cannons, which are quickly taking shape. The ballista is installed and a hole is cut for it to fire through.

The first test firing of the ballista is a good omen, as it hurls a box up over the garage rafters. A letter-gun, for firing envelopes, is built and tested. It works, but Jesse gives it the thumbs down: "The cool factor just wasn't there."

The trebuchet is mounted in the truck, necessitating only a small opening cut into the door for a perfect fit. A hole is cut into the roof for the air cannon and a linear actuator is installed to open and close the roof. When it's powered up, the roof lifts open without a hitch. Finally, Jesse mounts his giant truck-size exhaust smokestack, and it is time to test the beast.

The team takes the attack van to a nearby field, where all systems are pronounced GO. It's time for the challenge.

" I'm one of a handful of experts on ancient siege weapons in the world, so whenever anyone needs a working catapult, I usually get a call. The big problem with this job was the size. It takes a large machine to hurl a fifty-pound object one hundred feet. We had to fit a lot of machinery— the trebuchet, the ballista, and the air cannons—into a very tight space, and still have room to operate them safely. "

RON TOMS

The Monster Air Cargo van takes to the track—well, street: a quarter-mile residential drag strip where Jesse finds himself up against another delivery truck and a paperboy with a flair for speed. Soon newspapers and packages are flying through the air like laser-guided missiles. The outcome is close, but the Monster van wins. As the victor drives away, he lobs a free television set to a surprised customer; doubly surprised, as it arrives through his picture window.

MONSTER

Trebuchets were used in the Middle Ages to hurl plague-ridden corpses over castle walls, in the first recorded instance of biological warfare.

FACTOID

" We're putting a square peg into a round hole. "
DAVID NORRIS

JESSE'S FINAL THOUGHTS

"It was cool. It was cool to do something with the Mac Tools truck because there are so many Mac Tools dealers. There are about three thousand guys that drive those same trucks every day, so for them to see me smash trash cans and stuff, and then drive eighty miles an hour—they loved it."

COMING SOON TO A FOREST NEAR YOU

Pulp Friction

PT CRUISER WOOD CHIPPER

THE MISSION: TURN A CHRYSLER PT CRUISER INTO A HIGH-PERFORMANCE WOOD CHIPPER

" *This is like someone coming to my shop and asking me to build a moped.* "

JESSE JAMES

Team

JESSE JAMES

JOHAN BAKKER
Mechanical design engineer
BRIGHTON, MICHIGAN

PETE FINLAN
Custom painter,
car builder, and artist
VISTA, CALIFORNIA

MICK GIFFORD
Tree-chipper expert
WINN, MICHIGAN

TOM PREWITT
Custom motorcycle painter
BREA, CALIFORNIA

ERICH WOODALL
Master welder, fabricator,
and street racer
EDGEWATER, MARYLAND

MATT ZABAS
Artist, engineer, and fabricator
CARDIFF, CALIFORNIA

Specs

VEHICLE
2002 Chrysler PT Cruiser

ENGINE
Stock 2.4-liter DOHC 16 valve

TRANSMISSION
Stock 5-speed manual

**SUSPENSION-
BRAKES-STEERING**
EAI air-suspension system

WHEELS
#44 Jesse James

PAINT
By House of Kolor. Blended
black base coat, root-beer candy
base coat, and pagan candy
base coat under a clear coat.

MONSTER SPECS
Vickers vane-style Morbark
hydraulic pump, chipper housing,
chipper drum, knife holder, bottom
feed wheel; flame-thrower kit;
West Coast Choppers air cooler.

The Build

> " I know some people thought that it was not a big enough challenge, not adequate, or that it was too easy. I invite those people to come down here and try it. "
>
> JOHAN BAKKER

> " It's like a giant food processor. You just shove stuff in there and it spits it out the other side a couple of seconds later. "
>
> MATT ZABAS

he team follows the usual procedure of destruction before construction until the Cruiser is gutted. The first, and biggest, problem is space, or the lack of it. The chipper has to fit into 64.2 cubic feet of PT Cruiser space. Not easy if you've ever seen a Morbark 2070 XL Twister (you can take our word for it if you haven't). The unit consists of a chipper housing, chipper drum, knife holder, and bottom feed-wheel. The Twister is taken apart to be remade in a different configuration suitable for the Cruiser's size, and a sub-frame is added to handle the chipper's additional weight. When the chipper installation is complete, it comes within an inch of the Cruiser's outer body.

To make the back door hinge in reverse, the team removes the lift gate and fits it with a pelican hinge, effectively reversing the lift gate so that, when functioning, the closing lift gate will pull objects directly into the chipper's feed mechanism. Both engine exhausts are routed into the chipper discharge tube to give the beast a distinctive *ROARRRR.*

With the build completed, the team goes out for a test spin. They haven't made it very far when the lines to the air-bag suspension system lose pressure and fail, and the Cruiser sinks to the ground and cruises to a stop. Who had made the costly error of routing the air lines over the exhaust manifold?!?! (Don't ask, don't tell.) Eventually they arrive at a site where the chipper will be put to the test. The first thing it chews up and spits out is itself— pieces that were pulled off on Day One have become fodder for the newly crowned West Coast Chipper.

The Challenge

" *The chipper is a very unforgiving piece of equipment, a violent machine. It's a machine on the verge of explosion at any point in time. There's a lot of things happening inside. It's always amazing to see a big piece of wood go in and a little piece come out. To stand there and watch that, I mean, it's just a great feeling. I can walk through the woods and say there's nothing there that Morbark can't make into little pieces.*

"Taking a PT Cruiser and making it into a tree chipper is quite a concept. I think Monster Garage is on to something. Something engineers have never thought of in the past; combining two things into one. Maybe Monster Garage is building the better mousetrap today."

MICK GIFFORD

DANGER
NEVER Hand Feed This
Chipper For Any Reason

IT'S TOO LATE NOW!

COMPLAINT Department

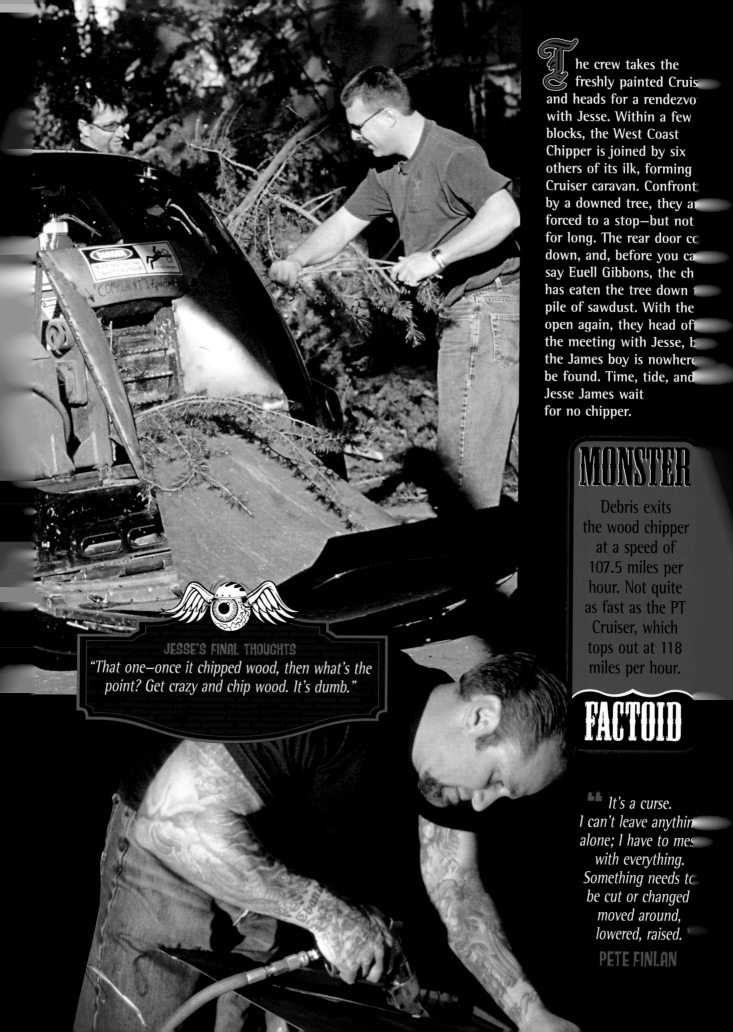

The crew takes the freshly painted Cruis[er] and heads for a rendezvo[us] with Jesse. Within a few blocks, the West Coast Chipper is joined by six others of its ilk, forming [a] Cruiser caravan. Confront[ed] by a downed tree, they a[re] forced to a stop—but not for long. The rear door co[mes] down, and, before you ca[n] say Euell Gibbons, the ch[ipper] has eaten the tree down [to a] pile of sawdust. With the [road] open again, they head off [to] the meeting with Jesse, b[ut] the James boy is nowhere [to] be found. Time, tide, and Jesse James wait for no chipper.

MONSTER

Debris exits the wood chipper at a speed of 107.5 miles per hour. Not quite as fast as the PT Cruiser, which tops out at 118 miles per hour.

FACTOID

JESSE'S FINAL THOUGHTS

"That one—once it chipped wood, then what's the point? Get crazy and chip wood. It's dumb."

❝ *It's a curse. I can't leave anythin[g] alone; I have to mes[s] with everything. Something needs t[o] be cut or changed moved around, lowered, raised.*

PETE FINLAN

THIS TRUCK HAS MORE MOVES THAN JAMES BROWN

Nut Shaker

THE MISSION, TAKE A FORD F-150 PICKUP AND TURN IT INTO A CONTRAPTION ALMOST NO ONE HAS EVER HEARD OF

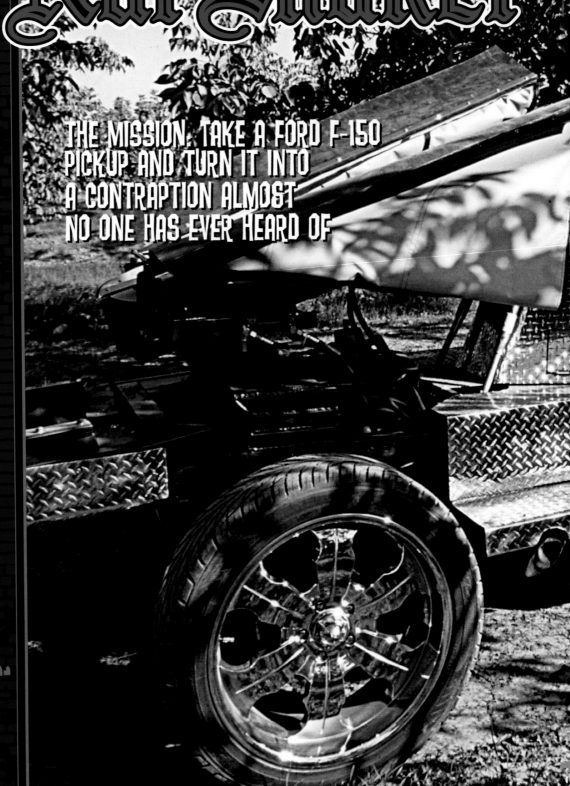

FORD F-150 PICKUP NUT SHAKER

" It can roll out to the nut farm, which is someplace I always thought I'd go. "

JESSE JAMES

Team

JESSE JAMES

RUSS ANGOLD
Agricultural engineer
SAN LUIS OBISPO, CALIFORNIA

TIM BEGHOEFER
Hydraulics technician and mechanic
MILWAUKEE, WISCONSIN

MIKE PITTINGER
Mechanical engineer
and underwater welder
BALTIMORE, MARYLAND

TOM PREWITT
Custom motorcycle painter
BREA, CALIFORNIA

DAN ROBINSON
Farm equipment repairman; welder
OMAHA, NEBRASKA

RALPH WESTERHOFF
Farm equipment service manager
TULARE, CALIFORNIA

Specs

VEHICLE
1997 Ford F-150 pickup truck

ENGINE
Stock 4.2-liter V-6

TRANSMISSION
Stock 5-speed manual

**SUSPENSION-
BRAKES-STEERING**
Stock brakes and steering.
Front coils replaced with
2,500-pound Firestone air-bag
units; rear springs converted to
four-link suspension.

PAINT
By House of Kolor.
Dark teal pearl shimmeron
with wood grain flames.

WHEELS
Alba Wheels

MONSTER SPECS
Orchard Machinery 800-pound
shaker head, conveyor belt,
hydraulic pump, hose, and motor.

The Build

❝ When I first heard about this challenge, I felt pretty confident. Little did I know. ❞

RALPH WESTERHOFF

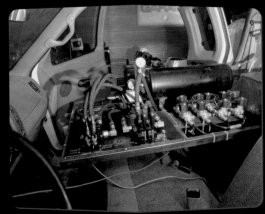

Before detailing the build, let's have Ralph Westerhoff explain exactly what it is that the team will be building: "A tree-shaker is a mechanical harvesting device for fruit and nut crops, a machine that clamps a tree trunk or limb and shakes the crop from the tree. Shakers are used throughout the world in tree crops, such as almonds, walnuts, pistachios, plums, and prunes, and even in fruit crops used in canning, like cherries."

The main component of any tree-shaking machine is something that does the shaking. In this case, it is an 800-pound hydraulic shaker head, custom made for Monster Garage by Orchard Machinery Corporation. The team removes the truck bed so that the shaker can be mounted directly onto the frame. In order to sustain the weight of the shaker, the frame is reinforced with steel. The rear suspension is converted to a four-link system, and the front coils are replaced with two 2,500-pound air-bag units.

Once the shaker head is affixed to the frame, the hydraulics to power it are assembled and installed. The power for the hydraulics will come from the truck engine.

A brushing adaptor for the hydraulic pump has to be machined, an eight-hour job that is accomplished at West Coast Choppers. The gas tank, which is too large to fit into the reconfigured frame, is cut down, welded, and then sent out to be sealed with a urethane lining. This seemingly simple act will have unforeseen consequences which might have cost the team dearly; urethane takes at least twenty-four hours to cure. The hydraulic installation, completed and ready for action, cannot be tested until the gas tank is ready.

On Day Five, the tank is installed and filled with gas, and all systems are go. When the shaker is powered up, however, it shakes like James Brown on a hot night in Georgia. The team has done the job with one day to spare—but wait: Jesse wants more. He informs the troops that not only does the shaker have to shake the nuts off the trees, it has to catch and store them as well. Day Six goes from calm to frenzy. A canopy, made from a parachute, is designed and fabricated. It will surround the tree, catch the nuts, and dump them onto a conveyor belt that will carry them to a small storage hopper.

The final test is carried out on a leftover Christmas tree. The shaker shakes, and ornaments fall into the canopy, onto the conveyor belt, and into the hopper. Bring on the walnut grove.

The Challenge

The challenge takes place in Tulare, California, the walnut capital of the world. Jesse and the Monster Shaker versus the vastly more experienced Ernesto aboard his 30-ton, 30-miles-per-hour commercial tree shaker. There is one walnut grove, from which each man will pick six trees to shake and harvest, then race to the finish line. Ernesto turns out to be a lot quicker than the oddsmakers figured, and it is neck and neck until the dash for the finish line, where the speedy pickup outguns the giant shaker.

MONSTER

With an annual harvest of one billion pounds, California has more nuts than any other state.

FACTOID

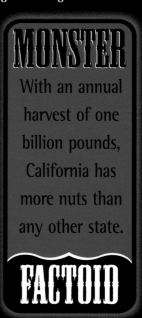

JESSE'S FINAL THOUGHTS

"I don't know about this one. Everybody loves it, but I don't know. The thing about it is, one guy made a bunch of pieces and then brought them in, so it was basically an installation job. I thought that if the place where he worked was making them, why couldn't we have just made it here? That's not happening again. It did look cool when it was done."

❝ The shoot was an interesting process. Coming into this, you have preconceived ideas about how it will go. As a fan of the show, having watched all the episodes before being asked to participate, I got the idea that some of what you see may be staged or camera magic, but I can tell you that it is all real. The design and build are left solely to the team. ❞

RALPH WESTERHOFF

MAKE MINE WITH MUSTARD, KRAUT, AND 1,000 HORSEPOWER

Hot Dogster

HOT DOG CART DRAGSTER

THE MISSION:
MAKE A TYPICAL
NEW YORK CITY
HOT DOG VENDOR'S
CART POP WHEELIES
AND DO 130 MILES
PER HOUR

Team

JESSE JAMES

TOM BETAR
Senior master tech
WEST NYACK, NEW YORK

STEVE BONGE
Classic customizer
NEW YORK, NEW YORK

MIKE DESMOND
Custom car designer
SOUTHERN CALIFORNIA

LOUIS DI RAIMONDO
Hot dog cart manufacturer
MIAMI, FLORIDA

DAN FERRAZZANO
Mechanic
PHILADELPHIA, PENNSYLVANIA

PETE FINLAN
Custom painter,
car builder, and artist
NEW YORK, NEW YORK

INDIAN LARRY
Motorcycle builder
NEW YORK, NEW YORK

DAVE TUCCI, JR.
Street rod fabricator
MARCY, NEW YORK

Specs

VEHICLE
2003 All American Hot Dog Cart,
Anniversary Special, and 1966 Woody
Gilmore slingshot dragster chassis

ENGINE
GM ZZ502 crate motor with Lyons
6-71 supercharger, Jeg's cam and
pistons, MSD ignition, and twin
Holley 750 CFM four-barrel carb

TRANSMISSION
B&M Racing & Performance Products

SUSPENSION-
BRAKES-STEERING
Custom steering.
Wildwood disc brakes.

PAINT
Pinstriping by Pete Finlan; Hot Dog
Designs

WHEELS
Original Gilmore dragster

MONSTER SPECS
Jesse James–fabricated exhaust
headers and pipes

Photo by Rick Scherer

The Build

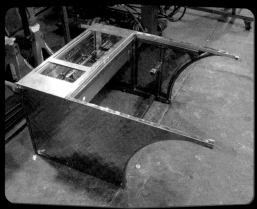

> I want to see a hot dog cart go 200— I want to see it in the air.
>
> **MIKE DESMOND**

ay One dawns bright and sunny, but the doors to Monster Garage remain closed as Jesse has a prior engagement over on Shoreline Drive, racing in the Celebrity Long Beach Grand Prix. (He finishes second.) This means that for the first time Design Day and Day One of the build are combined.

In order to combine a hot dog cart with a dragster, it helps to have one of each to work with. The hot dog cart is no problem; a model from Louis Di Raimondo's company, All American Hot Dog Carts, is in the garage awaiting its transformation. The dragster looks like a real problem until Jesse allows that he just happens to have a 1960s-era front-engine rail dragster in his possession.

As soon as the dragster arrives at Monster Garage, the crew sets about modifying it. The rails are shortened and the entire chassis is strengthened by welding in additional support struts. The front wheel assembly is welded into position. The first batch of parts arrives: fuel tank, tranny, front wheels, and rubber. The total cost is $2,894, leaving $106 for the rest of the build. From that point on it's freebies or failure.

The giant Mickey Thompson rear slicks will expand about four inches under load, so the hot dog cart is trimmed to take that into account. Everything goes without a hitch until it comes time to mount the tranny to the rear end assembly. The parts don't mate and there's not enough money left to purchase something that will work. Steve Bonge calls a friend, who says he can let them have something that might do the trick. Steve and Indian Larry go off to check it out.

The solution is to join the tranny and rear end with opposing yokes connected with a U-joint. The connection works. Next step: checking the old chassis welds. Every joint is gone over with a wire brush looking for cracks or other signs of failure. New welds are applied where needed and it appears the end is in sight when Jesse arrives with the exhaust headers he'd been working on. He takes one look at the U-joint coupling and says, "I'm not driving it like that." Given that the drive coupling was right between his legs, the crew immediately goes to plan B.

A new coupling is obtained and installed, and a shatter shield is fabricated to protect Jesse in case of unforeseen disaster. The engine (a freebie) is installed and the hot dog cart is attached to the rear of the dragster.

It's almost time to light up the engine, but first they have to install a wheelie bar at the rear to keep Jesse from pointing the nose skyward to the point of a back flip. Dave Tucci's ten-year-old son suggests taking the section of chassis that was cut off the front and relocating it to the back. Done.

Jesse places hot dogs—with buns—into the exhaust stacks, climbs in, and fires her up. With a mighty roar the engine fires, sending hot dogs flying all over the garage. The Hot Dogster is ready for action.

The Challenge

Photo by Rick Scherer

" I built a car for myself when I was fifteen. It was a 1963 Falcon that I eventually turned into a blown-alcohol drag car. Although the car was a rush, I felt that I could use my creativity more in the street rod field, so I started doing small fabricating jobs on street rods. I got more jobs than I could handle in my small garage, so we built the 6,000-square-foot shop we are currently in.

"I was able to drive the hot dog dragster back to the starting line after Jesse made his run. The car was awesome—all I could see was motor. I would have loved to have been able to make a pass myself, but watching Jesse leave the starting line was a close second. "

DAVE TUCCI

Photo by Rick Scherer

Photo courtesy of Steve Bonge

as Vegas Motor Speedway is the location. Jesse has the Hot Dogster lined up in front of the staging lights next to the Jeg's Mail Order Chevy Cavalier, driven by two-time NHRA Pro Stock World Champion Jegs Coughlin, Jr.

When the lights go green both machines light up the rears and blast down the quarter mile. The Jeg's machine tops out at 197.74, while the Hot Dogster crosses the line at 139.98 miles per hour. The first part of the race is over, but in the next phase the Dogster has the upper hand. While Jegs drives off to the concession stand to buy hot dogs for the crews, Jesse simply drives back to the start line and offers everyone a taste of the fastest hot dogs on the planet.

Jesse subsequently took the Hot Dogster to New York, where he was a guest on *Late Night with David Letterman.* With hundreds of Monster Garage fans lined up behind barricades, the planned live run down 53rd Street was aborted when the New York cops got wind of what was going on and shut them down. Jesse did, however, manage to get in one spectacular practice run.

MONSTER

In the early 1930s, dragster speeds topped 100 miles per hour. Today, a top fuel dragster can reach speeds of 320 miles per hour.

FACTOID

JESSE'S FINAL THOUGHTS

"It was wild. It's a handful trying to get the thing to go straight. I almost took out a phone booth when we ran it up in New York."

LIGHTS, CAMERA, WHACK!

THERE'S ALMOST AS MUCH ACTION BEHIND THE MONSTER GARAGE CAMERAS AS THERE IS IN FRONT OF THEM

We've all seen "behind-the-scenes" television shows about filming on a movie set. Lots of people stand around waiting for the director to set up the shot or call for action, while someone else yells "Quiet, please!" or "Quiet on the set!" That, most definitely, is not Monster Garage. If anything, the command that seems to prevail is: "Chaos on the set!"

It's true that Day One, the day the build design is finalized, is relatively calm—just Jesse and a couple of guys talking and sketching out ideas. The space where the designing takes place is constructed from steel scaffolding and set up above the floor of the garage. It's somewhat cramped and difficult to film in. While the Day One design progresses, the production crew not directly involved in the taping begins to get ready for Day Two, when everything changes—big time.

The first build day, Day Two, starts with the production assistants wetting down the garage floor with a garden hose, then turning on a smoke machine to set the mood for the familiar opening shot of the build team's arrival through the garage door. Jesse shows the team the vehicle, explains what the build has to accomplish, and turns the group loose to begin what will be a five-day orgy of noise: screeching metal, endless hammering, and raucous rock 'n' roll played on Jesse's boom box at a level loud enough to be heard over all of the other noise. Add in the sparks and flames that seem to erupt volcanically at various points in the room, the smell and sound of red-hot metal being ground to dust, and the unmistakable odor of welding torches, and you begin to feel as though you are a captive in some demented gearhead's idea of Dante's Inferno.

Welcome to another typical day at Monster Garage.

Monster Garage is a one-hour show; it's about 50 minutes without the commercials. So how many hours of Mini-DV high-definition tape do they shoot to get the requisite 50 minutes? According to Larry Law, a producer and editor who works at the post-production facility out in Glendale (at the corner, believe it or not, of Victory Boulevard and Jesse Avenue): "The average is about 80 hours, but I think they have hit 120 hours at least once. That would have been one of the record shoots. There will be three or four hours while they're working furiously, but not on anything visually useful or interesting. That stuff usually ends up on the cutting room floor. Basically, we have a six-week schedule. That

> **" We're not trying to change the world, just your oil. "**
> ### TOM McMAHON

pretty much takes it all the way to mixing it online and getting it out, which is very tight.

"When we get the show down to 60 or 70 minutes," Law says, "and it's looking really good, we then get to that heartbreaking period where you cut everything down to the bone, streamline it, and then have to lose things altogether to get the last few minutes out. It's frustrating because you want to keep this step-by-step thing in there and get the sense of the progression of the vehicle. Yet there comes a point where something has to go, and those are the really hard choices."

So with that sort of raw-to-finished tape ratio, is this a show that's made in the editing room? Producer Jeff Conroy says no: "It's a combination of the original concept, the actual shoot, and the edit. But the biggest part is what happens on the set. When you start off with a good concept, which basically never changes—to bury that concept will definitely bury the show."

How many production personnel does it take to shoot 80-plus hours of tape? There is a producer/director, plus an associate producer, a soundman, a production manager, two cameramen, two production coordinators, and two production assistants. Beyond this team, there's the post-production team and another, smaller crew that works for Alex Anderson, the garage honcho.

Most of the production crew had worked on other series or in television news, but none of them were quite ready for the Monster Garage thing, including soundman Ernest Saunders. "I've been on lots of sets in my day," Saunders says, "and this is about as loose as anything I've ever seen. The dynamics on the set change with every show. Every build is different. Sometimes you have a build with people who are jerks, but mostly the people are cool. You gotta go with the flow, keep an open mind."

For cameraman Dylan O'Brien the series has been a life-changing experience: "Before Monster Garage I did Discovery, History Channel, Modern Marvels, PBS stuff, but this is the most insane place I've ever worked in my life, and I love it. There's no way around it, it's crazy. Things happen here that don't happen on any other show. There are not too many places where you would take an ambulance and wheelie down the middle of traffic with it, or work in a place where there's fire, welding, explosions, more fire, and more welding every day, and it changes you. I remember on the hot air balloon, we had to test it in the middle of the night, and Jesse's out there in the driveway shooting 30-foot flames into the sky, everybody crazy, and the neighbors are looking out the windows. After a while it just becomes the normal thing, and you begin to think there's something wrong with the rest of the world."

Even series producer Tom McMahon, a 12-year veteran of NBC News, gets caught up in the Monster Mash: "This is the most unique experience I've ever had in television. It's by far the most fun. I love doing news, but this is really cool. It gets awful in here. It's dirty. You and the crew get totally whacked out. We've gotten very crazy down here. I can really feel the change that you go through in a week here—it's totally insane."

"My perspective," McMahon continues, "as the producer, not from a builder's perspective, it's just the coolest experience you could have to come here and really live through it with these guys. It's the ultimate guy show—cars, tools, burning things. It's a beautiful little bio lab—it's all dirty. We're not trying to change the world, just your oil."

Sometimes the noise, smells, explosions, burning, and other signature features of the Monster Garage experience ratchet up the tension meter. Emotions can run high in the latter stages of a build, so the crew begins to look for creative ways to blow off steam. This can involve racing radio-control cars around the garage, or racing bar stools, with gasoline engines mounted underneath, up and down the street. In one instance, champion hot dog gulper J. Marshall Cobe took on garage manager Alex Anderson and production coordinator Grace Bellamy in a hot dog eating contest. In the ensuing hand-to-mouth combat, Cobe won.

Music also is used to soothe the savage build-crew person. As in LOUD MUSIC. Local rock bands are invited in to play during some of the builds, but they need some pretty powerful amperage to overcome the ear-splitting din that passes for normal at Monster Garage.

One band, the Go-Nuts, had a cannon that fired a mixture of powdered sugar and caramel-coated popcorn into the air. Within minutes everything, including the camera and sound equipment, was coated in the stuff. The build, in which a crew comprised entirely of cops turned a patrol car into a donut shop, came to a screeching halt. The band came within an inch of being booked for felony littering with intent.

There have been other diversions: visits by actors, sports stars, police, firefighters, building inspectors, even the mayor of Long Beach. For the denizens of Monster Garage, it's all in a day's work. ◉

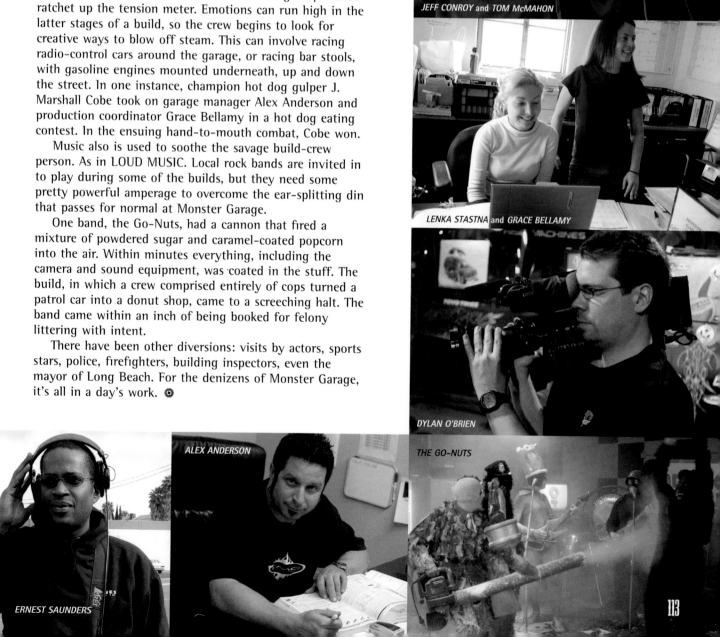

LARRY LAW

JEFF CONROY and TOM McMAHON

LENKA STASTNA and GRACE BELLAMY

DYLAN O'BRIEN

ERNEST SAUNDERS

ALEX ANDERSON

THE GO-NUTS

MONSTER GARAGE™

MUNICIPAL VEHICLES

FORD EXPLORER GARAGE TRUCK	LINCOLN LIMO FIRE TRUCK	AMBU-LANCE WHEELIE CAR	CHEVY SUBURBAN WEDDING CHAPEL

Your friendly neighborhood garbage can collector

WHITE TRASH

FORD EXPLORER GARBAGE TRUCK

THE MISSION:
TURN A FORD EXPLORER
INTO AN AUTOMATED
GARBAGE TRUCK

"*Because it's wrong.*"
JESSE JAMES

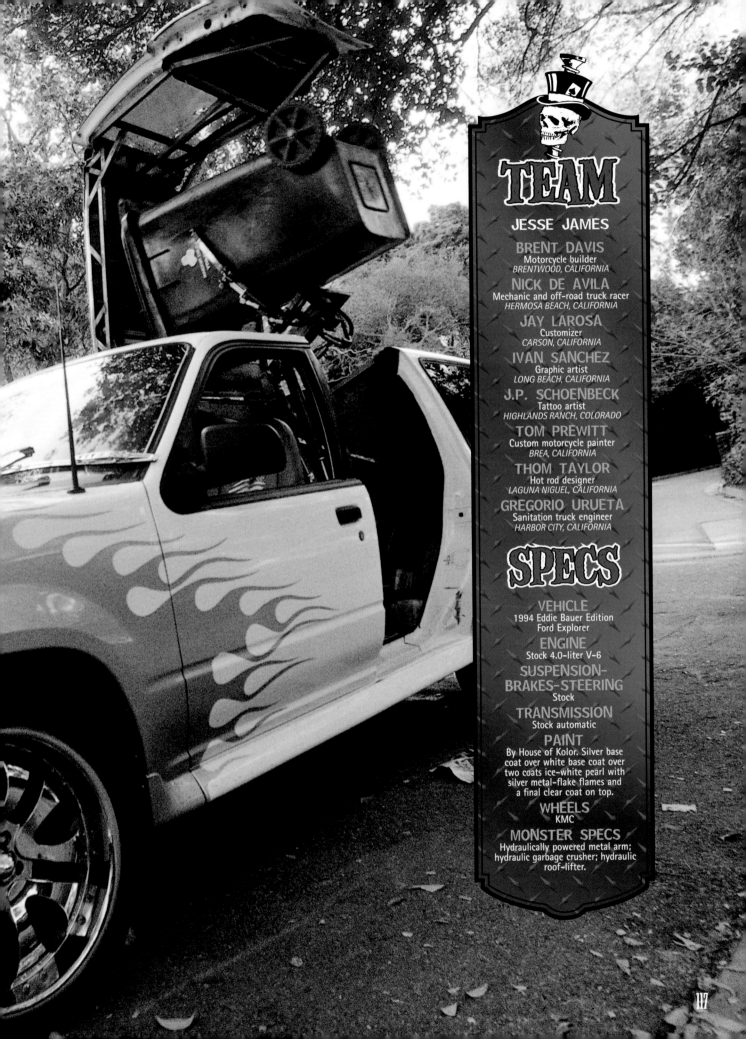

TEAM

JESSE JAMES

BRENT DAVIS
Motorcycle builder
BRENTWOOD, CALIFORNIA

NICK DE AVILA
Mechanic and off-road truck racer
HERMOSA BEACH, CALIFORNIA

JAY LAROSA
Customizer
CARSON, CALIFORNIA

IVAN SANCHEZ
Graphic artist
LONG BEACH, CALIFORNIA

J.P. SCHOENBECK
Tattoo artist
HIGHLANDS RANCH, COLORADO

TOM PREWITT
Custom motorcycle painter
BREA, CALIFORNIA

THOM TAYLOR
Hot rod designer
LAGUNA NIGUEL, CALIFORNIA

GREGORIO URUETA
Sanitation truck engineer
HARBOR CITY, CALIFORNIA

SPECS

VEHICLE
1994 Eddie Bauer Edition
Ford Explorer

ENGINE
Stock 4.0-liter V-6

**SUSPENSION-
BRAKES-STEERING**
Stock

TRANSMISSION
Stock automatic

PAINT
By House of Kolor. Silver base
coat over white base coat over
two coats ice-white pearl with
silver metal-flake flames and
a final clear coat on top.

WHEELS
KMC

MONSTER SPECS
Hydraulically powered metal arm;
hydraulic garbage crusher; hydraulic
roof-lifter.

MONSTER

Each year Americans discard 220 million car tires, 16 billion diapers, and 2 billion razor blades.

FACTOID

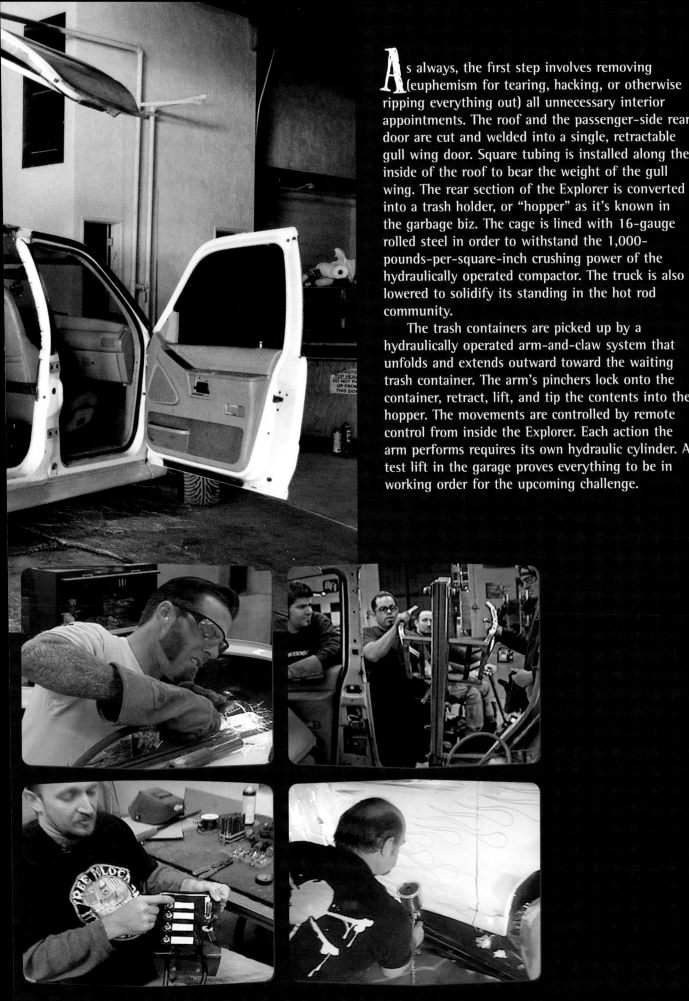

As always, the first step involves removing (euphemism for tearing, hacking, or otherwise ripping everything out) all unnecessary interior appointments. The roof and the passenger-side rear door are cut and welded into a single, retractable gull wing door. Square tubing is installed along the inside of the roof to bear the weight of the gull wing. The rear section of the Explorer is converted into a trash holder, or "hopper" as it's known in the garbage biz. The cage is lined with 16-gauge rolled steel in order to withstand the 1,000-pounds-per-square-inch crushing power of the hydraulically operated compactor. The truck is also lowered to solidify its standing in the hot rod community.

The trash containers are picked up by a hydraulically operated arm-and-claw system that unfolds and extends outward toward the waiting trash container. The arm's pinchers lock onto the container, retract, lift, and tip the contents into the hopper. The movements are controlled by remote control from inside the Explorer. Each action the arm performs requires its own hydraulic cylinder. A test lift in the garage proves everything to be in working order for the upcoming challenge.

> *"Lots of people make their living out of trash. So sometimes at work, when we smell the stuff coming off the trucks, we just say it smells like money."*
>
> GREGORIO URUETA

It's Jesse versus Los Angeles Sanitation veteran Henry Vaughn. One city block against the clock. Henry has the experience but his truck is big and cumbersome—time, 2 minutes 58 seconds. Jesse and the nimble Explorer take their turn: 2 minutes 32 seconds. Monster Garage does it again.

JESSE'S FINAL THOUGHTS

"Technically a hard one. We had to figure out a lot of hydraulic arms and stuff like that. I knew about hydraulics, but not how to make an arm or anything. I think no one on the crew really had a good grasp on it. And, everybody together, we powered through it."

Where's the fire?
HOT STRETCH

LINCOLN LIMO FIRE TRUCK

"I think we should go to the Oscars and squirt the paparazzi."

JESSE JAMES

THE MISSION:
TAKE A LINCOLN
TOWN CAR LIMOUSINE
AND TURN IT INTO
THE WORLD'S COOLEST
FIRE TRUCK

TEAM

JESSE JAMES

VINI BERGMAN
Custom limousine builder
CALIFORNIA

ED BLANFORD
Car designer
SOUTHERN CALIFORNIA

STEVE DENNISH
Hot rod creator
LA MIRADA, CALIFORNIA

WINK ELLER
Custom bike builder
ORANGE, CALIFORNIA

RICK GOODELL
Fire engine engineer
CLINTONVILLE, WISCONSIN

PAUL JOHNSON
Mechanic
TURLOCK, CALIFORNIA

LISA LEGOHN
Welding instructor
LOS ANGELES, CALIFORNIA

TOM PREWITT
Custom motorcycle painter
BREA, CALIFORNIA

MICHAEL SHROUT
Firefighter
LONG BEACH, CALIFORNIA

SPECS

VEHICLE
1996 Lincoln Town Car Limousine

ENGINE
Stock 4.65-liter V-8

TRANSMISSION
Stock automatic

**SUSPENSION-
BRAKES-STEERING**
Stock

PAINT
By House of Kolor. Base coat of
blue-blood red, two coats of ice-red
pearl, two coats of mini-fireball red
metal flake, one coat of fireball red
metal flake, two coats of candy-
apple red, and a coat of clear sealer.

WHEELS
KMC

MONSTER SPECS
Waterous Company fire pump and
nozzles; emergency lights; diamond-
plate step; chrome handrail; metal-
flake Naugahyde roof.

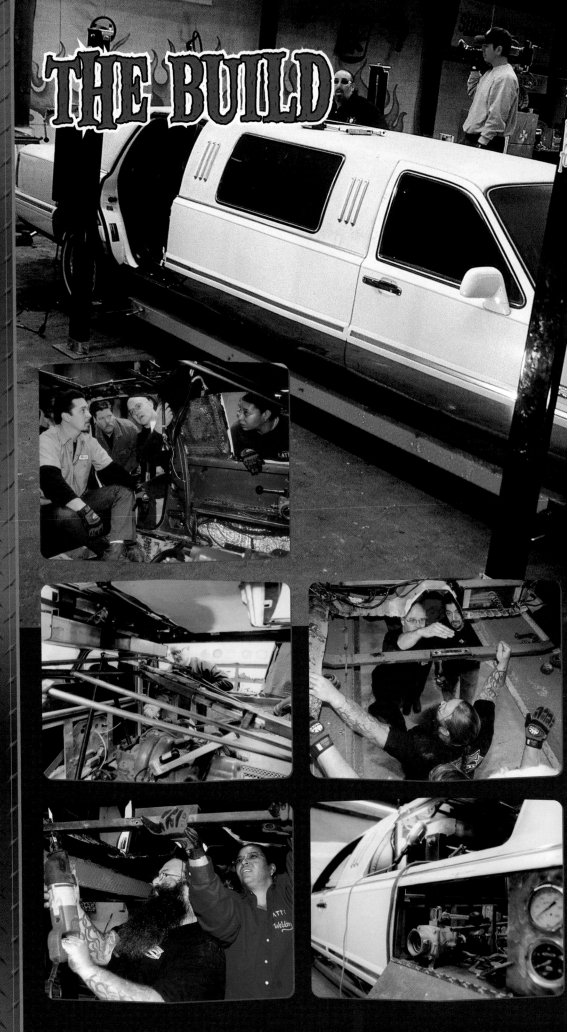

MONSTER

President George Washington was a volunteer firefighter. He joined the Veterans Fire Engine Company in 1774.

FACTOID

> "This isn't fluffy, fairy, foo-foo garage. This is Monster Garage."
>
> MICHAEL SHROUT

After the usual frenzy of tearing out the vehicle's innards, and a limousine has lots of innards, the team faces up to its biggest and most obvious task: installing a pump, powered by the limo's V-8, large enough to throw pressurized water more than one hundred feet into a roaring fire. Wait, let's modify that; first they have to find a pump. New high-velocity pumps retail for about $30,000, or ten times the entire budget.

Mike Shrout solves the problem by scrounging a used pump from a fire truck repair and salvage yard for only $1,500, or half the budget. There's one other significant pump statistic that has to be taken into account: its weight, 1,500 pounds. (Did Mike buy it by the pound?) To mount the unit, they must rip out the exhaust, extract the driveline, and cut a large hole in the 18-gauge steel floor pan. In doing that, they mistakenly cut through the lines that control the doors, switches, lights, and more.

They disconnect and drop the drive shaft out. It will be cut and modified to transmit power from the engine to both the pump and the rear wheels. The pump will be inserted into position from below, raised by a three-ton floor jack, then attached to the limo's frame. This is both delicate and dangerous. If the heavy pump falls, some of the crew won't be keeping time by snapping their fingers anytime soon. But it doesn't fall.

Since the engine power has to drive through the pump, the car will need two drive shafts. The rear shaft is removed and placed in front between the engine and the pump. It's a perfect fit.

The roof, which will open clamshell style to allow the water cannon ("monitor" in fire truck speak) and light bar to emerge from inside the limo, is sliced open with a Sawz-All. Rather than a hydraulic lift system, the crew decides to use an electric linear motor. It proves too weak for the job, so an ingenious system using garage door springs as a counterbalance is installed.

To make the pump system work, a special output shaft must be fabricated. Wink Eller goes to work on Jesse's turret lathe. After completing the shaft, he sculpts a custom-made protective housing for it from a chunk of solid aluminum.

With all the lines, pumps, motors, and other ancillary parts hooked up, the rig is given its first squirt test and passes, throwing a stream of water about 130 feet. When hooked to a hydrant, it will be capable of pumping over a thousand gallons a minute. Only the challenge remains.

THE CHALLENGE

MONSTER

In the 1st century B.C., the Roman fire department employed 7,000 firefighters.

FACTOID

THE CALL GOES OUT...ALL UNITS BE ADVISED. REPORT OF A STRUCTURE FIRE.

Two fire teams respond: The Long Beach Fire Department and The Monster Garage Volunteer Brigade. The Fire Department takes an early lead but is blocked by a stalled moving van in the middle of the street. The limo squeezes by and is first on the scene of the fire. The roof opens, the water cannon emerges, the hose is hooked up to a hydrant, and the limo begins pumping water onto the fire at a rate of twenty-five gallons per second.

JESSE'S FINAL THOUGHTS

"That one, I think, was easy. The whole thing that Wink made, the roof and the light bar flipping, was cool, but putting the pump in line with the drive shaft and running all the plumbing through that, I don't think was really that hard. The crew will probably be bummed to hear that, but I didn't see a big challenge in it."

A high-speed attack
RESCUE 911

FABU-
LANCE
WHEELIE
CAR

" *I know now why God put me on this earth— to pop wheelies.* **"**

JESSE JAMES

THE MISSION:
TO ACCELERATE FROM
0 TO 60 IN 5 SECONDS
WHILE RISING INTO
A FULL WHEELIE

TEAM

JESSE JAMES

JOSH BROWN
Designer and custom car fabricator
HEMET, CALIFORNIA

MIKE DESMOND
Custom car designer
MARYSVILLE, CALIFORNIA

DAVID DYSON
Paramedic and custom parts maker
FREMONT, CALIFORNIA

DARRELL FERGUSON
Cell phone field engineer and
custom car fabricator
EL SOBRANTE, CALIFORNIA

RICHARD PAUZA
Designer, fabricator, and
custom-hot-rod builder
GILBERTS, ILLINOIS

TOM PREWITT
Custom motorcycle painter
BREA, CALIFORNIA

RICHARD SCHROEDER
Wheelie car expert
DIAMOND BAR, CALIFORNIA

SPECS

VEHICLE
1983 Ford E-350 XL
Type II ambulance by
Wheeled Coach Industries

ENGINE
460 Ford from Wayne's Engine
Rebuilders with Edelbrock heads,
cams, intake manifold, and 750cfm
carburetor. Speed parts by Jeg's.

TRANSMISSION
Stock Ford C-6

SUSPENSION-
BRAKES-STEERING
Rear axle welded to frame. Front
brakes removed, rear fitted with
CNC turning brake. On four
wheels—stock steering with power-
assist removed; while in
wheelstand—hand-operated brake
steering.

PAINT
By House of Kolor. Snow-ice pearl-
white on a snow-white pearl base
with stripes of tangelo pearl over a
lemon-yellow and molly-orange mix
base, with flames of ultra-orange
and sunrise pearl.

WHEELS
BAZO

MONSTER SPECS
V-drive custom built by Casale
Engineering. 400-pound weights
welded into the back to provide
extra wheelie ballast.
Titanium-tipped scraper bars;
custom-fabricated roll cage; Cobra
racing seats. Window tinting by
Mike's Tint Shop.

THE BUILD

> *To do a good wheelstander, you are usually talking at least three to five months.*
>
> RICHARD SCHROEDER

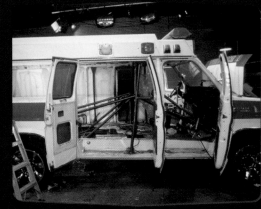

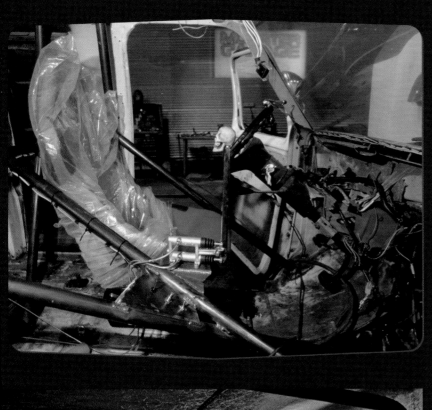

There's a lot of stuff inside an ambulance, as the team discovers when they go to tear it all out: cabinets, wood flooring, paneling, insulation, medical equipment. They produce the biggest pile of junk in the history of Monster Garage.

The chassis is reinforced and a double-hoop roll bar internal cage is made and installed to aid rigidity and help handle the enormous amount of torque that will be generated. In order to put as much weight as possible behind the rear axle, the engine and transmission are moved and reinstalled, facing backward. This allows the axle to act as a fulcrum, enabling the front to rise into the air when Jesse floors the gas pedal. It's a monster job, taking the better part of the build. An internal, inverted chassis and mount for the engine and tranny are fabricated and installed. A custom-made V-drive gearbox, normally used in high-speed boats, is the critical linkage allowing the engine's power to turn back around to the rear axle passing via a short drive shaft into the V-drive, back out the V-drive, and down through another short drive shaft into the rear end. The dashboard is removed and a hole is cut through the lower front of the ambulance so that Jesse can see where he's going during the wheelstands.

The engine must be capable of delivering 300 horsepower and 350 foot-pounds of torque. On Day Six the 19-year-old, 200,000-mile stock motor is replaced by a 460-cubic-inch racing engine. Jesse fabricates and installs eight flame-belching exhaust stacks. All that remains is the lift-off.

THE CHALLENGE

Jesse

Jesse and the team go to Irwindale Speedway for a 1/8-mile drag race against a stock fire rescue ambulance. During Jesse's first trial run, a fire breaks out in the back of the wheelie ambulance. Fire crews and medics rush to his aid, but Jesse waves them off. Fire or no fire, he is there to race. After assuring the team that he is not going to be immolated, he orders the crew to "fire it up." The two ambulances take their places, the Christmas tree goes from red to green, and the race is on. Jesse pops a wheelie and roars down the track for the win. He celebrates by doing wheelstands until he runs out of gas.

MONSTER

Each year the New York City Fire Department makes more than 1.2 million ambulance runs. That's one every 30 seconds.

FACTOID

JESSE'S FINAL THOUGHTS

"This was the best. No other car, unless we build another wheelie car, will ever compare to the ambulance."

Unlawfully wedded
4X4 VOWS

CHEVY SUBURBAN WEDDING CHAPEL

THE MISSION:
TAKE A CHEVY SUBURBAN,
TRANSFORM IT INTO
A WEDDING CHAPEL,
AND FIND A COUPLE
WILLING TO GET
MARRIED IN IT

> "I want
> it loud."
> JESSE JAMES

TEAM

JESSE JAMES

DONALD BURNES
Ordained minister
SOUTHERN CALIFORNIA

TONNA CARLO
Hot rod painter and fabricator
OLYMPIA, WASHINGTON

JOHN FRYE
Car designer
TORRANCE, CALIFORNIA

TONY GENTILE
Custom-hot-rod builder
TUJUNGA, CALIFORNIA

STEVE HOSKING
Certified electrical, mechanical,
and computer engineer
SANTA CRUZ, CALIFORNIA

CHARLES KEGG
Pipe organ builder
CLEVELAND, OHIO

RAY KENT
Theater technical director
ALISO VIEJO, CALIFORNIA

JIM MORRISON
Industrial contractor and
hot rod builder
SALEM, OHIO

TOM PREWITT
Custom motorcycle painter
BREA, CALIFORNIA

SPECS

VEHICLE
1994 Chevrolet Suburban C2500

ENGINE
Stock 5-liter V-8

TRANSMISSION
Stock automatic

SUSPENSION-
BRAKES-STEERING
Stock

INTERIOR
Red velvet door panels and driver's
seat by Willy's Upholstery. Tinted
windows by Mike's Tint Shop.

PAINT
By House of Kolor. KS212 metallic
silver primer, IPO2 ice-white pearl
base coat, MF-2 silver miniflake,
then F-15 silver flake and clear
coat. Stained glass: candy-apple red
and pagan gold, blended.

WHEELS
KMC Venom wheels with Spintek
Vegas spinners

MONSTER SPECS
Birdseed thrower powered by a 12-
volt motor and four actuators; two
300-pound-capacity Accel linear
actuators; one Accel 500-pound
heavy-duty actuator; custom copper
and aluminum calliope pipes; Kepp
organ keyboard.

THE BUILD

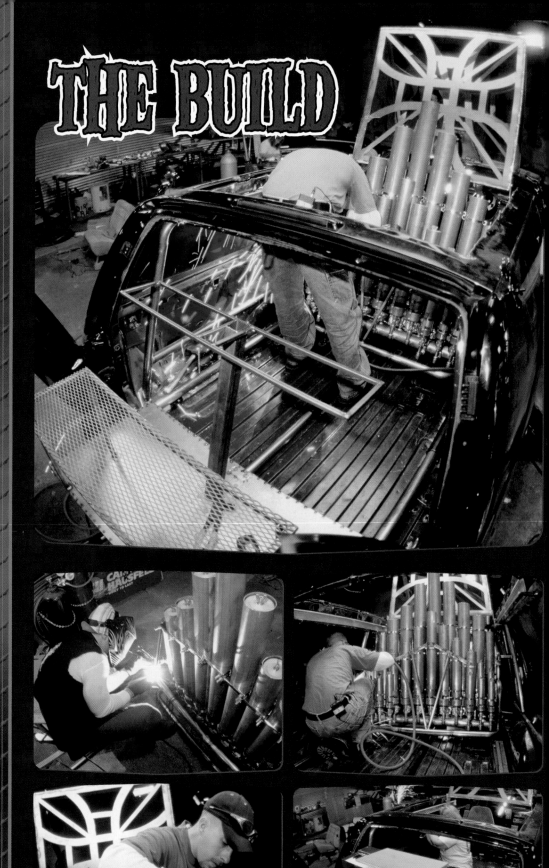

"Jesse wants a total monster and we're going to do everything we can to give it to him."

STEVE HOSKING

136

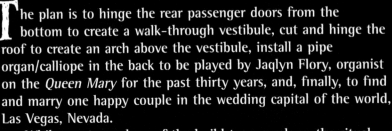

The plan is to hinge the rear passenger doors from the bottom to create a walk-through vestibule, cut and hinge the roof to create an arch above the vestibule, install a pipe organ/calliope in the back to be played by Jaqlyn Flory, organist on the *Queen Mary* for the past thirty years, and, finally, to find and marry one happy couple in the wedding capital of the world, Las Vegas, Nevada.

While most members of the build team work on the ritual vehicle gutting, Steve Hosking goes off-site, where he will spend most of the build period working on a lathe to make the pipes and construct the organ.

Using a large piano hinge, the rear doors are successfully remounted into a reverse gull wing configuration and hooked up to the linear actuators that raise and lower them. A platform to mount the still unseen calliope is constructed, and panels are added to the inside of the doors to permit the happy couple to walk into the monster chapel. The panels are so heavy that the actuators can no longer move the doors. The time that is lost due to this problem, and the arguments over who was responsible, almost cause a couple of the crew to sue for divorce, or at least a trial separation. Once the doors are lightened and functioning properly, the mood inside the garage begins to improve—but not for long.

Jesse fabricates a tube-steel swing to hold the finished calliope pipes, allowing them to lie flat for driving, then swing up for the nuptials. Once the Maltese Cross arch that Tonna designed and cut is installed, there is nothing for the team to do until Hosking delivers the calliope. As tensions are once again reaching the boiling point, the calliope pipes arrive and the assembly process begins. A frame is built into the passenger seat space for the nitrogen tanks that will power the calliope, and the birdseed thrower is fabricated and installed.

After the pipes are installed in the swing, using clamps designed and welded by Jesse, the swing is installed, lined up, and tested. It works. In fact everything works except the calliope; that's still being massaged by Hosking, who is wiring the keyboard and plumbing the nitrogen. Tony, who earlier had popped his top at Tonna over the weight of the doors, vents his anger at Steve for the speed, or lack thereof, in assembling the calliope. With time rapidly running out, the calliope is completed and put to the test by Ms. Flory. It sounds like it was tuned using no known musical notation—but it works.

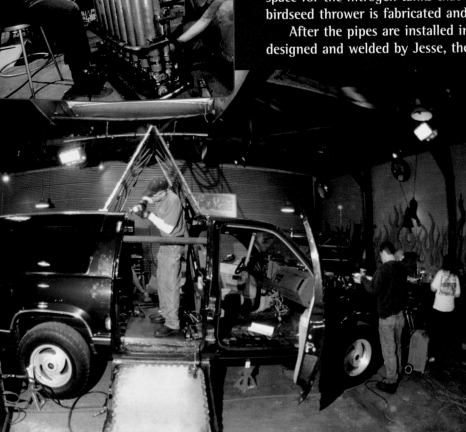

THE CHALLENGE

The whole concept of a roll-around pop-up wedding chapel is pretty outrageous. I'm sure most of my colleagues in the business would have turned their backs and said these people are totally insane, which, for the record, they are. "

CHARLES KEGG

CHRIS AND SARAH WADE aka...THE HAPPY COUPLE

"We had our original wedding planned for May 24. It was going to be very traditional, totally the opposite of what we did in Vegas. The whole thing started as a kind of joke. We were dealing with a ton of stress and one night Chris saw the commercial on television about getting married by 'the man,' Jesse James. He told me what we could win and I said OK, thinking we would never win.

"We entered on Monday and every day afterward until that Friday he called my cell phone trying to disguise his voice, leaving me messages saying that we had won. He totally thought we would win. I thought it would be awesome, but never really gave it any chance.

"Then one Saturday night the phone rang, and I ran into the bedroom. He said I was standing there shaking and my mouth was on the floor. According to him, I gave him the phone while I ran around saying 'Oh, my God!' over and over. I was really freaked out and thought how surreal this was and then called every living soul I knew to tell them we had won. Only a few people knew that Chris had entered us. My dad knew and he thought we were lying. Chris's family kept saying, 'Only you would win something like this; only you.' Chris's friends, who all ride bikes with him, went ballistic. We had no second thoughts."

The Discovery Channel arranged for a private ceremony to be held in the garden area behind the Stardust Hotel prior to their filmed wedding. In addition to family and friends, Jesse and the production crew were in attendance. Sarah continues:

"Although the actual Monster Garage ceremony presided over by Jesse lasted five minutes max, we filmed for about four hours. It was so fun. The chapel rocked. We loved the stained glass, the automatic doors, and the pipe organ. What wasn't to love about it? Once we finished, the crew got everything done and met us. We partied until about four in the morning. Wow! Jesse was definitely an interesting minister. Very unorthodox, but very cool, aside from the fact that he asked Chris if he would take me as his 'Old Lady.'

"We had the best time. I don't think any bride, or couple for that matter, enjoyed their wedding day as much as we did. For us it was a perfect day. We would do it again in a minute. We're going back to Vegas next year for our anniversary and are inviting the whole production crew to come with us."

JESSE'S FINAL THOUGHTS

"I don't know about that one. The crew was running a little lean. I didn't know until I watched the show when it aired that they were doing all that stuff behind my back. I had no idea, so I guess that's cool."

With the one-of-a-kind mobile wedding chapel finally operational, it's time for it to fulfill its destiny: marry a couple in Las Vegas on Valentine's Day. In typical Hollywood fashion, a scenario is devised whereby a potentially happy couple—who just happen to be in tux and gown and are disconsolate over their inability to find anyone to marry them in a city that performs more than 100,000 weddings a year—are "discovered" by Wayne Newton. Newton immediately calls Jesse. Thanks to the Internet, Jesse is a newly ordained minister, and before you can say "I do," they do, and the deed is done.

The Discovery Channel had held a week-long sweepstakes to see if they could find a couple willing to be married in this somewhat unorthodox manner. Out of the 9,000 couples who said "we will," Chris Wade and Sarah Kilborn from Charlotte, North Carolina, were selected. Chris, a former Marine, is a twenty-nine-year-old college student studying business management, and Sarah is a twenty-eight-year-old high school Spanish teacher.

ANYTHING YOU CAN DO
THE WOMEN OF MONSTER GARAGE

Of the more than one hundred and fifty welders, fabricators, electricians, and others who worked on the builds covered in this book, eight were women.

For television-commercial director Carol Hodge, working in a mostly male environment, as she did on the Switchblade build, was nothing new:

"I've always worked with men, always kind of preferred working with men. Growing up with brothers, I guess I feel more comfortable being around guys. This is all about teamwork. It's the first time I've ever welded. It's really fun. Anything involving sending sparks shooting and melting metal, it's great."

Christy Sumner, a Hollywood special-effects technician, also felt perfectly at home in the testosterone-fueled garage environment during the Swamp Buggy build:

"I was always a tomboy, always into sports, into building things with my dad, who was a carpenter at heart. My grandmother actually built furniture and my mom has always been very creative. I think it was just something that I grew up with and I loved, but I don't really dig working on cars. I don't like the mess and my hands always getting ripped up. On the other hand, I would do any job with these guys. I would love to have them on my crew. We all got along really well—never any tempers flying when things got hot and heavy under the hood. It was just, let's figure out the problem, let's figure out the puzzle; and that's exactly the way it has to be in my job. You can't lose your cool."

Hodge and Sumner are both "take charge" women who are successful in traditionally male-dominated fields. That's true for the other women as well: Tonna Carlo (Wedding Chapel episode) is an automotive painter and fabricator; Laura Parker (Stock-Car Sweeper) is a welder and art teacher; J'me Whitlock (Delivery Van) is a welder; and Wendy Schmidt (Golf Ball Collector) is an animatronics specialist. Animatronics? Here's what Schmidt says:

"I do mechanics and electronics. Other people design the puppet, an animal or a monster or whatever—what it's going to look like—and they tell me how much space I have to work with and what it is they want it to do, and it's my job to make it do that. I'm also a grip; I do lighting for the film industry, which involves a lot of rigging. I like things to move and I like to know how

> " I don't look at them as male and female. I look at everybody as a function—you know, like a tool to help me get the thing done. And if the tool doesn't work, then I don't care what gender they are. A couple of women who have come in here whomped on the men. "
>
> ### JESSE JAMES

things work. My dad was a carpenter and my grandfather was a mechanic, so I've had a love of tools since I was a small kid. I used to take apart all the little mechanical trucks and save the motors and try to rewire them to do other things. I had a blast when I was on Monster Garage."

Renee Newell (Zamboni episode) is both a sculptor and a certified welder who has worked on her share of heavy industrial jobs:

"As the only woman in a shop situation, you definitely get a little bit more attention. It kind of makes you a bit more sensitive to things. I'd rather not get the extra attention, unless I did something—a great weld, or I had a great idea; not just guys going, 'Oh, can I help you?' or 'Let me pick that up.'

"The reason I got involved in welding is that I do metal sculpting. I apprenticed for an artist and he suggested I take some classes. I did, and I loved it. So I went to the next level and got certified."

Newell's instructor at the Los Angeles Trade Technical College was a woman named Lisa Legohn. That's the same Lisa Legohn who would later impress Jesse during the Fire Truck build. "Lisa was good," says Jesse. "She's funny and a pretty good welder—you know, above average." In Lisa's words:

"I began welding when I was in high school. I took a welding course sort of as a joke, but when I got into it I enjoyed it. The whole aura of welding captivated me. It's metal, it's rugged and tough, but then with a little heat you can shape it and change it and it's all bright and shiny. I was fascinated with the things you can do with steel. I knew then that I was going to be a welder.

"Jesse's really nice—like a big kid who has all these fantastic toys and doesn't know what to do with himself. He's awesome at what he does. I'm a tradesperson and I respect the artistry of his work. The welds on his bikes are incredible. But everybody kisses up to him, and I was like, 'Excuse me?' I told him, 'The only difference between you and me is you have more money—but I weld better.'"

Her laughter as she recalled that moment captured her experience on Monster Garage as well as or better than anything put into words. "I used to be very shy," she added, "and would never say anything like I do today. But I'm a cancer survivor—three years in remission—and I look at life differently now. I let it out." ◉

Carol Hodge

Wendy Schmidt

J'me Whitlock

Lisa Legohn

MONSTER GARAGE

FORD MUSTANG LAWN MOWER

CHEVY IMPALA ZAMBONI

STOCK-CAR STREET SWEEPER

PORSCHE GOLF BALL COLLECTOR

A CUT TO THE CHASE
SWITCHBLADE

FORD MUSTANG LAWN MOWER

THE MISSION:
Turn a Ford Mustang into the world's fastest lawnmower

"If I'm a halfway intelligent person golfing and I see a five-liter Mustang coming with straight pipes and chrome lawnmowers coming out of the side, I'm going to let him play through."

JESSE JAMES

TEAM

JESSE JAMES

GEORGE BEERS
Parts guru
STUART, FLORIDA

BOB CLEVELAND
Racer and lawnmower engineer
LOCUST GROVE, GEORGIA

MIKE CONTRERAS
Oil rig mechanic
LONG BEACH, CALIFORNIA

MIKE DESMOND
Custom car designer
MARYSVILLE, CALIFORNIA

BILL DODGE
Custom bike builder
LONG BEACH, CALIFORNIA

CAROL HODGE
Television commercial director
SEATTLE, WASHINGTON

BILLY LANE
Custom bike builder
MELBOURNE, FLORIDA

TOM PREWITT
Custom mototrcycle painter
BREA, CALIFORNIA

SPECS

VEHICLE
1990 Ford Mustang GT

ENGINE
Stock 5.0-liter V-8

TRANSMISSION
Stock automatic

**SUSPENSION-
BRAKES-STEERING**
Stock Ford

PAINT
By House of Kolor. Lime-green
pearl base coat under ice-gold
pearl with lime-green metal flake,
followed by two coats of lime-
green candy apple. "Kameleon"
green-to-silver flame details
with a clear coat over all.

WHEELS
Gold wire-rims

MONSTER SPECS
10-horsepower Briggs and Stratton
lawnmower engine; 48-inch Delta
deck mower; three cylindrical
rotating blades.

THE BUILD

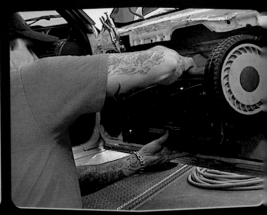

"The car we're using is some sixteen-year-old girl's 'Daddy gave it to me' car, and we're going to gangsterize it and make it this monster that kills grass."

BILL DODGE

CUSTOMER PARKING &
AUTO BODY SERVICES

147

on a floppy disk. It's nice to be a part of that, particularly when so many young people are going the other way. Most of them see it as where the opportunity is; but I think it's the other way around."

BILLY LANE

00:18:33

00:32:05

00:33:30

`00:30:25`

Jesse, the team, and the Mustang Switchblade travel to West Coast Turf in Indio, California, for a mow-off against turf pro Daniel Torres and his 4,000-pound tractor mower. The big tractor takes an early lead, but once Jesse gets Switchblade fired up it is no contest. He passes Torres doing 70 miles per hour, cutting every blade in his path. Monster Garage is the king of the turf.

JESSE'S FINAL THOUGHTS

"That one was cool, the first episode. I don't know, I trip out when I watch that one now. It seems so long, years ago. It's still the same deal; the purpose is pretty raw. We didn't have any idea what we were on to."

MONSTER

A square foot of lawn has 3,000 blades of grass. A single grass plant has 387 miles of root.

FACTOID

CHEVY IMPALA ZAMBONI

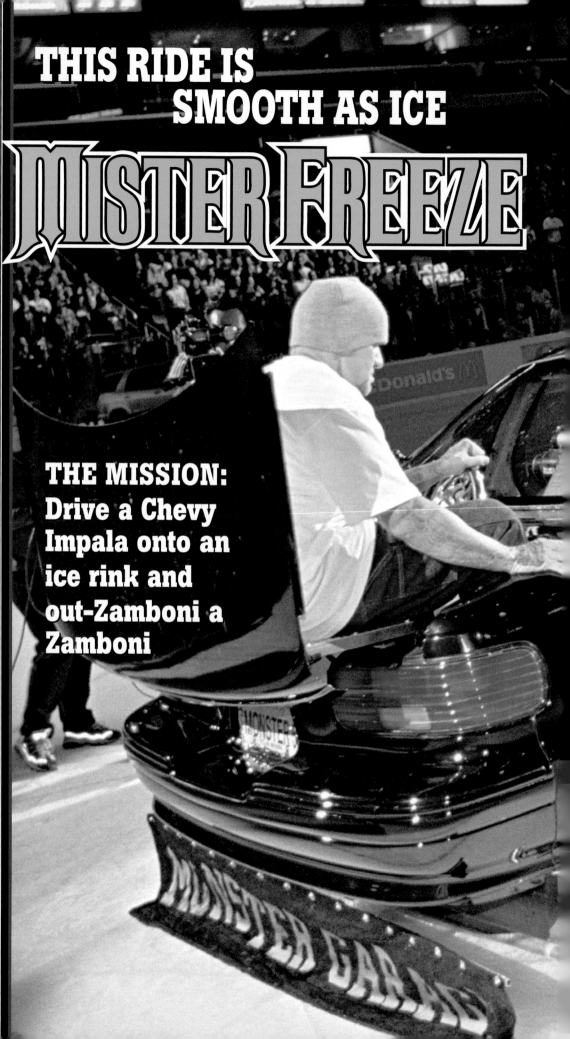

THIS RIDE IS SMOOTH AS ICE

MISTER FREEZE

THE MISSION:
Drive a Chevy Impala onto an ice rink and out-Zamboni a Zamboni

" *This project is kind of like having Henry Ford help us build a Model A.* "
JESSE JAMES

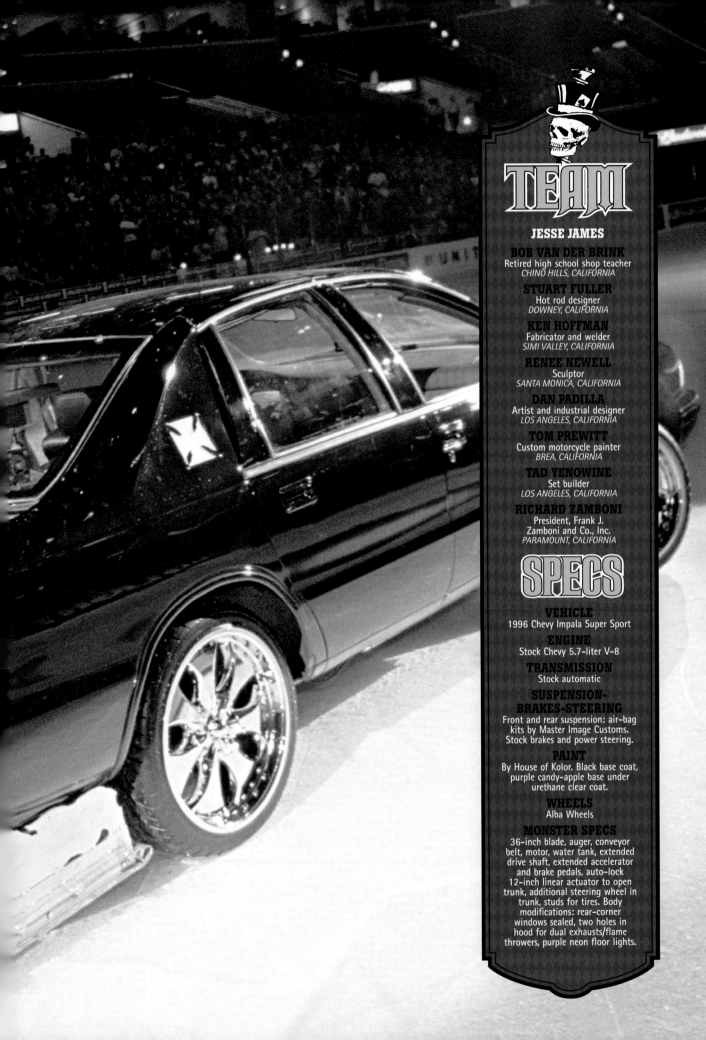

TEAM

JESSE JAMES

BOB VAN DER BRINK
Retired high school shop teacher
CHINO HILLS, CALIFORNIA

STUART FULLER
Hot rod designer
DOWNEY, CALIFORNIA

KEN HOFFMAN
Fabricator and welder
SIMI VALLEY, CALIFORNIA

RENEE NEWELL
Sculptor
SANTA MONICA, CALIFORNIA

DAN PADILLA
Artist and industrial designer
LOS ANGELES, CALIFORNIA

TOM PREWITT
Custom motorcycle painter
BREA, CALIFORNIA

TAD YENOWINE
Set builder
LOS ANGELES, CALIFORNIA

RICHARD ZAMBONI
President, Frank J.
Zamboni and Co., Inc.
PARAMOUNT, CALIFORNIA

SPECS

VEHICLE
1996 Chevy Impala Super Sport

ENGINE
Stock Chevy 5.7-liter V-8

TRANSMISSION
Stock automatic

**SUSPENSION-
BRAKES-STEERING**
Front and rear suspension: air-bag
kits by Master Image Customs.
Stock brakes and power steering.

PAINT
By House of Kolor. Black base coat,
purple candy-apple base under
urethane clear coat.

WHEELS
Alba Wheels

MONSTER SPECS
36-inch blade, auger, conveyor
belt, motor, water tank, extended
drive shaft, extended accelerator
and brake pedals, auto-lock
12-inch linear actuator to open
trunk, additional steering wheel in
trunk, studs for tires. Body
modifications: rear-corner
windows sealed, two holes in
hood for dual exhausts/flame
throwers, purple neon floor lights.

MONSTER

An average ice rink contains 10,211 gallons of frozen water.

FACTOID

" It's got kind of a funny name, it's not Smith or Jones. My dad, who invented it, called it an ice-resurfacing machine and then, after a number of years, everyone was saying, 'Here comes the Zamboni.' It was amazing to him. "

RICHARD ZAMBONI

THE BUILD

A Zamboni has these essential components: a sharp blade to scrape the ice and an auger that brings the ice to the center; a conveyor belt with paddles that brings the ice into the machine and drops it into a container; and a water tank that drops water behind to make new ice.

The crew begins by getting rid of everything inside the car that doesn't say "Zamboni." The rear end is essentially gutted, with the trunk lid, rear window, bumper, and taillights removed. Jessie cuts the floor out of the trunk to make room for the rear-seat steering compartment. This seat has to rise up far enough for Jesse to see over the top of the roof while driving the vehicle on the ice. This relocation of the steering also means extending the brake and accelerator pedals, rigging a new steering box and column extensions, and rerouting all of the appropriate fluid and electrical lines and control cables. A frame is constructed to reinforce the trunk, and hinges are fabricated and installed for the pop-up trunk lid.

Jesse visits the Zamboni factory and comes away with some all-important used parts: a blade, an auger, and an old rusted belt and paddles. Back at the garage a support frame is fabricated under the rear frame to support the blade and auger. The blade is mounted on two steel runners to slide it smoothly across the ice. A starter motor powers the auger and paddles. A water tank, which would subsequently prove too small, is installed inside a fabricated steel tank and PVC plumbing is attached to drop the water onto the ice. A new 8-gallon gas tank replaces the larger original 20-gallon unit. Finally, studded tires are made using sheet metal screws; the resulting holes are sealed with Slime. With forty minutes to spare, the "Slamboni" takes to the ice and the team members get their tool boxes.

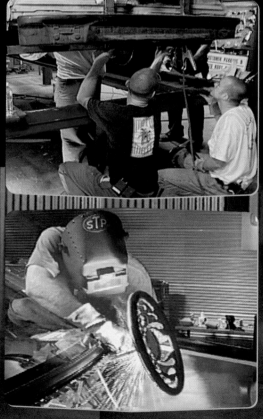

"People have a tendency to look down their noses at kids in the shop classes. California, and lots of other states, are phasing out shop classes because it's not politically correct to get your hands dirty. My whole statement about that is real simple; it comes from an article in Motor Magazine: A group of kids are talking and Kid One says, 'What are you going to do when you graduate?' Well, Kid Two answers, 'I'm going to trade school and be a mechanic.' Kid One says, 'With your grades you can go anywhere you want'; and Kid Two's answer was that 'without a good mechanic, nobody goes anywhere.'"

BOB VAN DER BRINK

At the Staples Center in Los Angeles, it's Jesse in the Slamboni versus the Zamboni factory machine. About a thousand Los Angeles Kings fans are on hand to see Jesse take on the Zamboni but, as Monster Garage executive producer Thom Beers explains, things did not go exactly as planned:

"Boy, did we take a beating at the Staples Center. The real Zamboni hit the ice and rumbled to its starting position. Then the beautiful deep purple and chrome Impala Super Sport rolled out onto the ice. Our build team went into action, making the final preparations for the race. One of them turned the gravity-feed water spigot on and waited while the introductions were made and the production crew got into position. Minutes rolled by, and while Jesse waited for the green flag to drop, gallons of tepid water poured out of the spigot and onto the ice. The water and the tires, still warm from sitting on the concrete backstage floor, did what they do, and the Impala SS slowly...melted...into...the...ice."

Needless to say, the challenge is rescheduled. Round Two of Slamboni vs. Zamboni goes off without a hitch and ends in the first and only dead heat in Monster Garage history.

X E100S 18 TX E100S 19 TX E100S

18A 18 19A 19 20A

JESSE'S FINAL THOUGHTS

"That one was cool, because before we started that one I had no idea even what a Zamboni did. I thought it was just dumping water on the ice."

MONSTER

Before the Zamboni it took three men, a horse, and a scraper one hour to resurface a rink. A Zamboni completes the task in just ten minutes.

FACTOID

STOCK-CAR STREET SWEEPER

"If I hit the wall because of something they screwed up, they're not going to feel the pain—until I catch them."

JESSE JAMES

CLEAN SWEEP

THE MISSION:
Sweep up dirt
and debris at
160 miles an hour

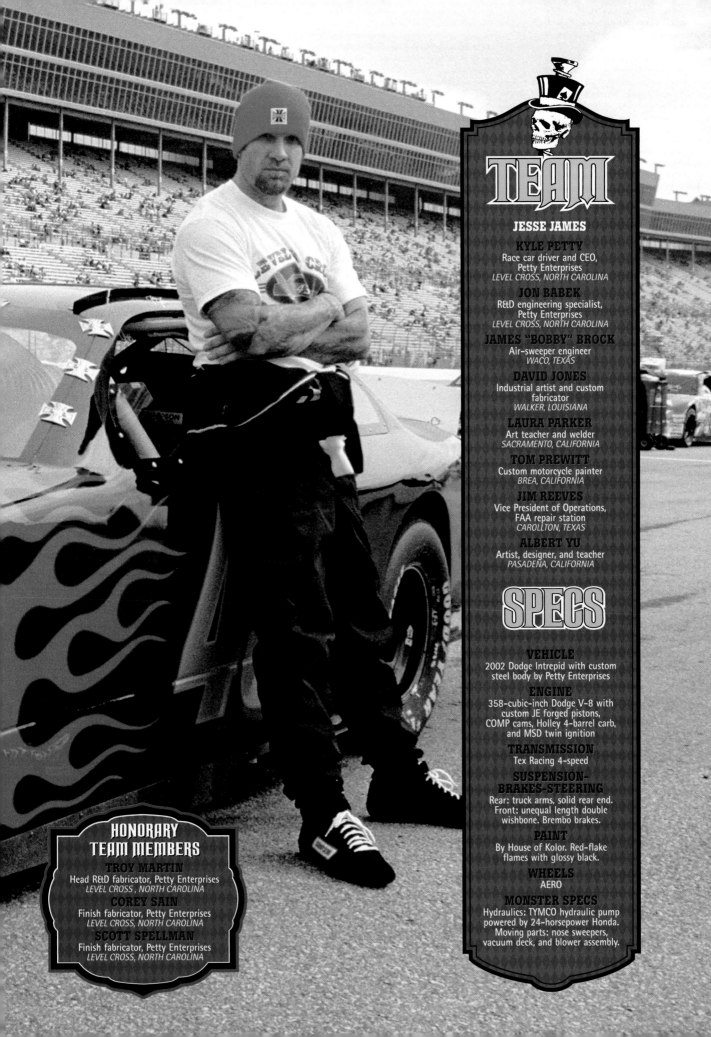

TEAM

JESSE JAMES

KYLE PETTY
Race car driver and CEO,
Petty Enterprises
LEVEL CROSS, NORTH CAROLINA

JON BABEK
R&D engineering specialist,
Petty Enterprises
LEVEL CROSS, NORTH CAROLINA

JAMES "BOBBY" BROCK
Air-sweeper engineer
WACO, TEXAS

DAVID JONES
Industrial artist and custom
fabricator
WALKER, LOUISIANA

LAURA PARKER
Art teacher and welder
SACRAMENTO, CALIFORNIA

TOM PREWITT
Custom motorcycle painter
BREA, CALIFORNIA

JIM REEVES
Vice President of Operations,
FAA repair station
CAROLLTON, TEXAS

ALBERT YU
Artist, designer, and teacher
PASADENA, CALIFORNIA

SPECS

VEHICLE
2002 Dodge Intrepid with custom
steel body by Petty Enterprises

ENGINE
358-cubic-inch Dodge V-8 with
custom JE forged pistons,
COMP cams, Holley 4-barrel carb,
and MSD twin ignition

TRANSMISSION
Tex Racing 4-speed

**SUSPENSION-
BRAKES-STEERING**
Rear: truck arms, solid rear end.
Front: unequal length double
wishbone. Brembo brakes.

PAINT
By House of Kolor. Red-flake
flames with glossy black.

WHEELS
AERO

MONSTER SPECS
Hydraulics: TYMCO hydraulic pump
powered by 24-horsepower Honda.
Moving parts: nose sweepers,
vacuum deck, and blower assembly.

HONORARY
TEAM MEMBERS

TROY MARTIN
Head R&D fabricator, Petty Enterprises
LEVEL CROSS , NORTH CAROLINA

COREY SAIN
Finish fabricator, Petty Enterprises
LEVEL CROSS, NORTH CAROLINA

SCOTT SPELLMAN
Finish fabricator, Petty Enterprises
LEVEL CROSS, NORTH CAROLINA

THE BUILD

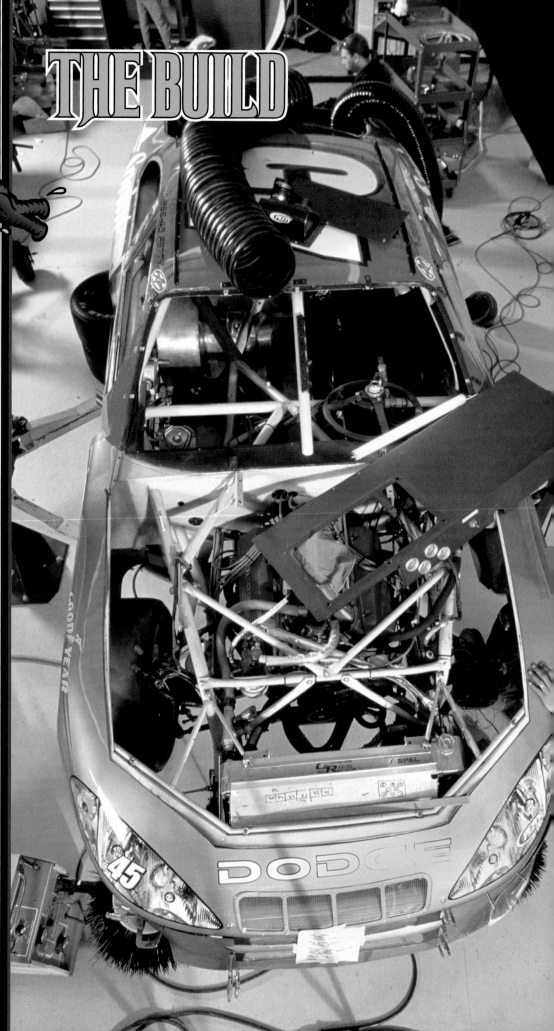

> " It's pretty neat to be in the Petty garage. I know people that would sell their children to be here right now. "
>
> **DAVID JONES**

Unlike a normal (normal?) build where the vehicle is immediately gutted, the race car construction of the Petty Dodge left precious few "unnecessary" parts. Under the supervision of Petty team engineers, the fuel cell is removed and the bottom rear trunk area is exposed to make room for the blower housing unit and the sweeper hopper.

The sweeper's heart is a giant fan, powered by a 24-horsepower Honda motor. On one side of the blower housing unit, air is sucked into the system and debris caught in this air stream is captured; on the other side, air is blasted out onto the street as if by a giant blow-dryer.

The build team fabricates a housing under the hood to support the sweeper brushes, then mounts the sweeper-broom mechanism and fabricates a new front hood assembly that will open at high speed without causing the car to crash. The Honda motor is installed and the blower fan is mounted into a fabricated steel housing. To lift the housing at high speed, a pickup head mechanism is designed and welded into place below the trunk area. The blower fan is attached to eight-inch tubes, which are then attached to the blower housing and pickup head. The Honda engine/pulley system that powers the hydraulics used to turn the sweeper brushes is installed. The hopper chamber is fabricated and installed, the hydraulic lines are hooked up, and the world's fastest street sweeper is almost ready for its maiden test run. Almost ready, because the Petty team engineers and mechanics have to perform a complete nuts-to-bolts inspection to make sure the car is ready for the racetrack.

With just minutes of build time left, the crew takes the high-speed sweeper out into the Petty parking lot. There, with only 4 minutes and 40 seconds to spare, it does the job, picking up a pile of crushed cans.

"Shooting the show off-site in our shop was a first for Monster Garage. There were many logistical problems, especially since we still had to build race cars during the shoot. One of the greatest things about being an engineer is seeing a project from the initial drawing—whether it's on a napkin or drawn on a piece of paper by an artist—clean through until the end when it is tested. Our plan was to finish on time. Once we were committed, I was sure that it would be done on time and work properly."

JON BABEK

The showdown comes at Atlanta Motor Speedway: Jesse in the Petty sweeper versus TYMCO's flagship Model 435 sweeper. Each vehicle must pick up two separate piles of crushed cans that have been placed out on the track, and Jesse has to do two laps to just one by the TYMCO sweeper. A racing official drops the green. Jesse and his 750-horsepower machine are quickly up to speed, sweeping through the turns, picking up cans. One lap. Two laps. The checker falls. It's Jesse by a broom.

MONSTER

The only parts on a NASCAR stock car that are actually "stock" are the roof, the front hood, and the deck lid.

FACTOID

JESSE'S FINAL THOUGHTS

"That one was good. I kept thinking for sure that The King or Kyle was going to come into the race shop at any second and say, 'What are you guys doing? Stop, stop.' They were totally into it. It was awesome to drive. I did a little over 170 on the backstretch. I came out of turn four at about 150, and I stepped on it a little too hard and got sideways. That got my attention."

DRIVING THE RANGE

PORSCHE GOLF BALL COLLECTOR

" It's got to be like a weapon. "
JESSE JAMES

THE MISSION:
Turn a Porsche 944
into a high-class
range-picker

TEAM

JESSE JAMES

ALEX ANDERSON
Custom car builder
TEMECULA, CALIFORNIA

MAC GILLUM
Range-picker builder
STANTON, CALIFORNIA

PETE PEPE
Creative animation designer
LOS ANGELES, CALIFORNIA

TOM PREWITT
Custom motorcycle painter
BREA, CALIFORNIA

ERIC SCARLETT
Custom car builder
VENTURA, CALIFORNIA

WENDY SCHMIDT
Animatronics specialist
LOS ANGELES, CALIFORNIA

JAY SKWARLO
Bicycle builder and mechanic,
and hot rodder
LONG BEACH, CALIFORNIA

SPECS

VEHICLE
1984 Porsche 944

ENGINE
Stock 151-cubic-inch 4-cylinder

TRANSMISSION
Stock 5-speed, rear transaxle

**SUSPENSION –
BRAKES–STEERING**
Stock Porsche

PAINT
By House of Kolor. Black base
coat and urethane clear coat,
blue pinstriping with ultra orange
pearl and sunrise pearl flames.

WHEELS
Polished Porsche stock

MONSTER SPECS
Gull wing doors powered by
300-pound AutoLoc electric
actuator; 100-volt motor-driven
golf-ball conveyor; animatronic
golf-ball clown eyes; three-barrel
nitrogen-powered golf-ball cannon;
5-gallon EAI chrome tank;
Jax Bicycles sprockets and chains;
custom wing.

THE BUILD

"*If there's a problem, I think on maybe the fourth day we'll light the car on fire and just, you know, cook marshmallows or something.*"

ERIC SCARLETT

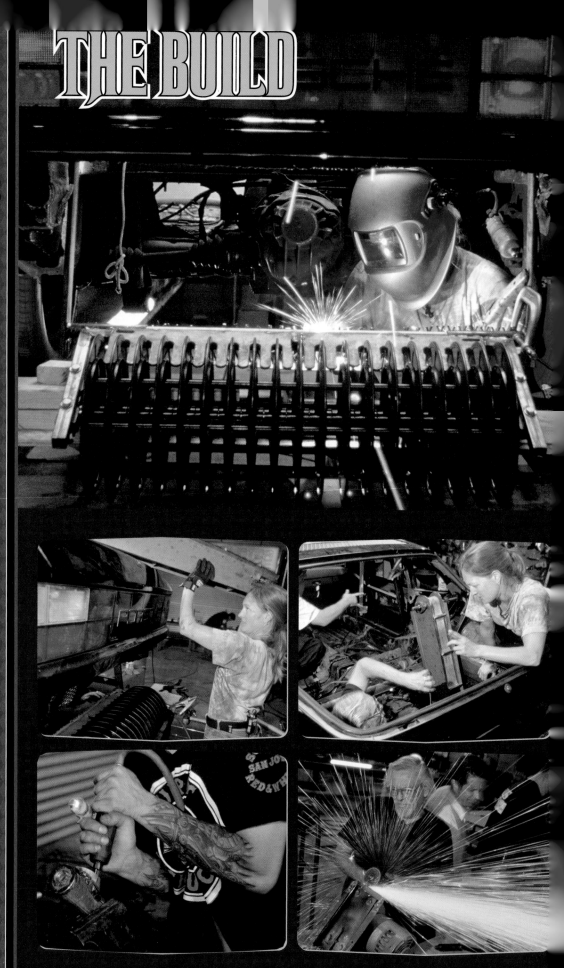

164

The front passenger seat comes out to make room for the golf-ball cannon while the rear seats are removed to accommodate the picker mechanism and the ball-conveyor system. The window glass is removed, to be replaced with steel mesh. The crew divvies up the work and sets to it. After removing the rear bumper, truck floor, and fuel tank, it's discovered that the Porsche's rear transaxle will severely limit the space available for the picker and the ball-conveyor mechanism. The passenger door is removed, lightened, and reinforced. Difficulty with the installation of the activator that will lift the door is solved by Jesse, and, with new hinges welded on the top, the gull wing flies.

The picker will lift the golf balls off the grass and feed them to the conveyor. The conveyor will feed them to a basket and the basket will feed the cannon. The golf-ball cannon is the creation of Eric Scarlett. After several failed tests, he finds the right combination of loading angle and pressure, then fabricates a fully functional system. A steel cage is constructed for the ball transport system. Problem: The balls are bunching up at the entrance to the conveyor. Solution: Install a small crossbar to force the balls to ascend in pairs. The lever and cable system intended to lift the picker stops short of the needed height. The arm for the power window is quickly adapted to do the job and all is right with the world. Jesse attaches the cool rear van wing he's fabricated, and the Porsche is almost ready for its debut. Based on Jesse's design, Wendy fabricates a frightening steel clown face with animatronic eyes that disguise the ball cannons. Once this is in place, they're off to the driving range.

THE CHALLENGE

> "Just getting this sucker to pick up golf balls on its own is quite a feat. Then you ask us to take it from one point, elevate it two feet in the air, gravity-feed it back down again, and then you want it to shoot a golf ball two hundred yards out into the fairway—you don't bother asking too much, do you? The reason I'm so proud of the group is that they pulled it off. To tell you the God's honest truth, I could take this same crowd and build any damn thing you wanted to build."

MAC GILLUM

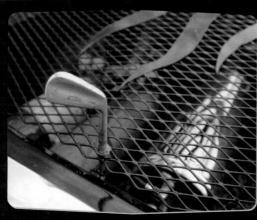

The duffers at the El Dorado Park Golf Course driving range have no idea what the day holds in store for them. Jesse wheels onto the range, picking up balls at an alarming rate of speed. The golfers try their best to hit the speedy Porsche until Jesse stops, raises the roof, and unleashes the cannons. In a few minutes, it is all over as the astonished hackers, unable to believe their eyes, flee for cover.

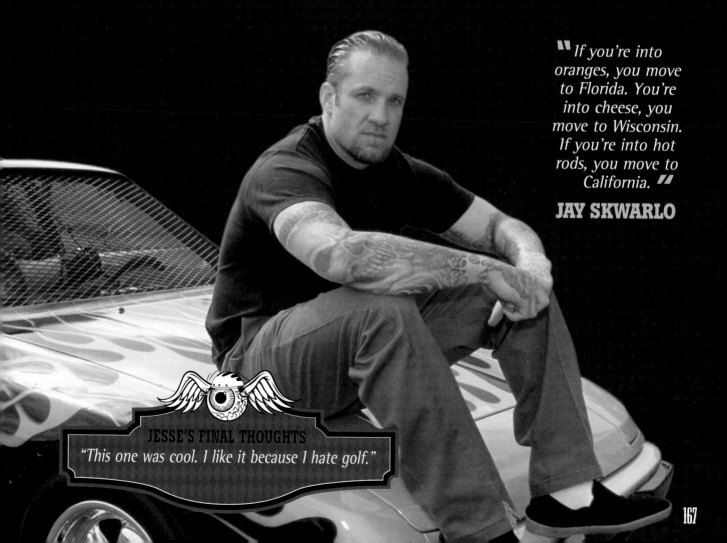

"*If you're into oranges, you move to Florida. You're into cheese, you move to Wisconsin. If you're into hot rods, you move to California.*"

JAY SKWARLO

JESSE'S FINAL THOUGHTS
"*This one was cool. I like it because I hate golf.*"

THE SAGA OF THE GRIM RIPPER 2

R.I.P.
"I hate losing."
JESSE JAMES

TEAM

JESSE JAMES

GEORGE BARRIS
Legendary custom-car designer
LOS ANGELES, CALIFORNIA

TIM CONDER
Mechanic and
motorcycle customizer
SEATTLE, WASHINGTON

JOSE GONZALEZ
Forklift repairman
and motorcycle customizer
LONG BEACH, CALIFORNIA

BART GRANDE
Dyno shop owner and racer
OCEANSIDE, CALIFORNIA

DORAN HIRSCHKORN
Manufacturing engineer
BISMARCK, NORTH DAKOTA

STEVE STERLE
AKA TOMBSTONE
Horror prop manufacturer
SAN FERNANDO VALLEY,
CALIFORNIA

In the first year of Monster Garage there are twenty-two episodes, each with the potential for one sort of catastrophe or another. Yet only one vehicle doesn't make it out of the garage. Only one team doesn't get the job done. The vehicle in question starts out as a 1973 Miller Meteor Cadillac Hearse. It's estimated that this hearse carried about ten thousand people to their final resting places. The task is to turn this grim reaper into:

The Grim Ripper

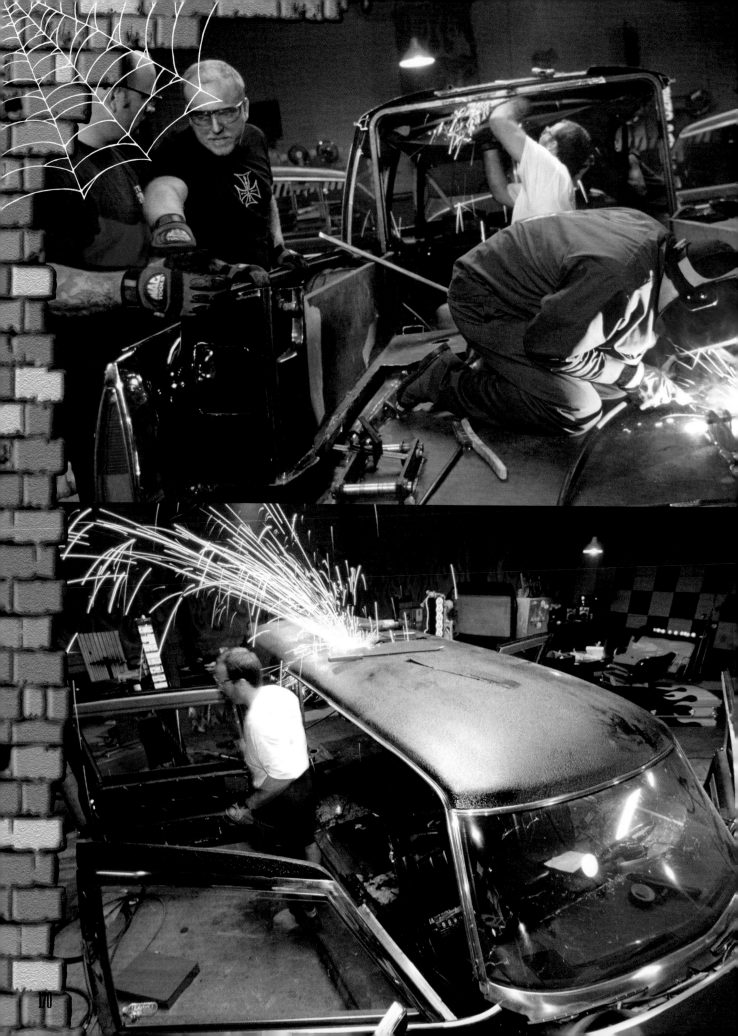

The concept is a good one: Build a monster that is equipped to cripple any car caught in its path. This will be done with two giant 600-pound Bobcat hydraulic arms that rise up out of the Ripper's roof to rip through the hood and metal framework of any car. An auger welded to the Ripper's rear will drill through any vehicle coming at the hearse from behind.

But it's not to be. The effect of the extra-heavy roof is underestimated, and the plan to operate the hydraulic pumps (that would power the Bobcat arms) by running them off belts attached to the engine is fatally flawed. "There were," builder Bart Grande explains, "two major technical challenges, the first being my responsibility, which was mounting the hydraulic pumps. I underestimated the load these pumps would be under and therefore kept burning belts. The second challenge was the folding roof. Our team did not have much experience or depth when it came to structural design and engineering, and therefore we wasted a lot of time re-engineering the roof design. To sum it all up, I believe there was a lack of teamwork."

Here is how series producer Tom McMahon looks back at the build: "The team had a lot of fun. It was a really hard build and I think they totally got suckered in by how hard it was. They were working right down to the end. When that thing was working, five minutes before midnight, they were scrambling—hydraulic lines were breaking, they were burning through fan belts. Then, finally, we had this huge fire. It was kind of climaxed by the fire. They were sitting in the hearse, just totally hammered and beaten, coming up with really dumb, totally unworkable ideas—just desperate. Finally, one guy goes, 'Jesse, what do you think?' It was like the ultimate moment. Jesse turned and didn't do anything. He just sat there and really kind of bent down and said, 'I think we failed.' It was like, 'Oh, my God, we're failing. This is weird, what are we doing? We failed. Everything is like ninety percent done, nothing's finished; I should have worked you guys harder. I take full responsibility. I hate failing.' Then he got up, put his motorcycle helmet and jacket on, and rode out of the garage. The team was in shock. They hadn't really considered failure. They were all looking deep inside. It was totally heavy—amazing. It shocked me. I never expected it to be that intense. I couldn't have scripted that one better."

What do you do with a failed Monster Garage creation, a hearse no less? As a fitting finale for a vehicle that has carried so many others to the end of the line, the hearse is loaded onto a flatbed truck and transported to the appropriately named Terminal Island. There, it is dropped into a car crusher and destroyed in a giant pyrotechnic display worthy of some Wagner opera.

There is another theory as to why this particular build failed. It has to do with the hearse itself. Were the souls of those who took their final ride in it disturbed in some way? More than one person has said of Monster Garage that the noise level inside is enough to wake the dead. Could it be that this time it actually did?

JESSE'S FINAL THOUGHTS

"I don't know. Right from the design phase, I don't think it ever really got fully started. The design was pretty vague and the crew was more interested in being on TV than they were in working. I thought for sure that Thom Beers was gonna make me come back in the next week and finish it, and we'd just fake it or something like that. When I called and told him, 'Man that thing didn't make it, the guys didn't get it done, it caught on fire,' I took the blame for it. I thought for sure he was gonna say, 'Well, we gotta finish it.' But, he said, 'Oh my God, that's awesome.' He thought it was great because he knew it would be great on TV."

"I got to live with this, man. I live in Long Beach. I'm going to see all these people and they're going to look at me and go, 'There's the guy that didn't finish that project.' I'm screwed."
JOSE GONZALEZ

"To come up short really hurts, man. I won't lie to you."
DORAN HIRSCHKORN

CAR 54, WHAT ARE YOU?

THE TIME HAS COME TO MAKE THE DONUTS

As Jesse and the gang gear up for the second season of Monster Garage, they decide to try one of the more unusual ideas that was kicked around at an earlier planning session—to take a classic black-and-white police patrol car and turn it into a donut shop.

With the exception of a couple of guys who know their way around a donut, the crew is made up of current or retired police officers. The plan is simple: On Day One they will design; on Day Six they will make and eat the donuts; on Day Seven they will arrest Jesse.

The design team is comprised of artist Jason Hurst; Long Beach Police Officer Frank Torres; Jay Hillebrandt, a service technician for Belshaw Brothers, Inc., a maker of donut machines; and Alan Dively, a product development technologist for Dunkin' Donuts. Jesse starts things rolling with a mission statement.

"The purpose of this build," Jesse says, "is to provide a public service. Everybody knows that cops love donuts, so we're going to add more time and get more mileage out of our tax dollars by bringing the donuts to them instead of having them take time off from fighting crime to go get donuts. If they have them right there all the time, they can still bust people."

After a quick denial from Officer Torres, they get down to work. Jesse suggests splitting the car down the middle with one half remaining a patrol car and the other a donut shop. This will allow room for a perp to be placed in the rear seat. That idea falls foul of reality when Alan Dively and Jay Hillebrandt begin to explain just how much equipment will have to be squeezed into the car in order for it to make the donuts. Words like cooker, fryer, hopper, mixer, conveyor, glazing, and shortening are being lobbed back and forth by the donut mavens like

tennis balls at Forest Hills. Jesse, using pure Monster Garage logic, suggests a decisive course of action. "Do we want to have a bad guy in the car," he asks, "or donuts? I want donuts."

Alan Dively knows from experience that making donuts is no piece of cake. "Despite what people may think," he says, "making donuts is a pretty complicated process. The technology is always changing, people come up with new ingredients that improve the donuts dramatically—it's kind of like computer technology."

Given the size and complexity of the donut-making equipment, it is decided that a final decision as to location and installation will wait until the car is gutted; in other words, Jesse's to be precise: "This is gonna be harder than I thought. We're gonna have to wing it."

On Day Two the build crew arrives in the usual manner with backlight and lots of fog, but with one major difference from the crews from earlier episodes: These guys are armed. They are: Mike New, Jr., a deputy sheriff from Suffolk, Virginia; John Pytlovany, the chief of police in Scotia, New York; Brian Armstrong, a police officer from Long Beach, California; and Randy Villata, a retired police officer from Los Gatos, California. Jay Hillebrandt from the design team returns for the build phase. As the only member of the team who knows donuts from the other side of the counter, he will, as Brian Armstrong explains, immediately take a central role in the project:

"On the first day we basically told each other the kind of experience each of us had, and with Jay it's kind of special because he works for the company that makes the machinery. He knows how the machinery sets in, so it's kind of, he says, 'Hey, I've got to have this here and that

here to make this work.' You know, kind of 'Do this and that because I need that part for my machine to work,' and we go off and make the part and then lay it in there and it's done."

Jay Hillebrandt, who is a fan of the show, is somewhat surprised by the real thing:

"I'm a fan of Monster Garage and Junkyard Wars and all the shows where they tear something up and make something else out of it. It's great. Now that I'm here it's just a little bit tougher than we thought it was going to be. I mean, there's a lot of work we put into that car. The toughest two things were the splash shield for the fryer and the rear door."

Given the level of difficulty, the build goes smoothly and without any frayed egos. This, it is generally agreed, is due to all of the builders being in the same profession. All except Jay, of course, but by the end of the build he is, as Brian explains, just one of the troops. "I think that since we all have the same thing in common as far as our careers," Brian says, "it definitely helped us bond together as a group. Jay is just a great guy to get along with, really knowledgeable with his company's equipment, and excellent at welding on stainless steel. He's kind of like us, too—he's right in there doing the work, so that's something we have in common even though he's not in law enforcement."

As the build nears its completion, the long hours begin to take their toll, particularly on Randy and John, the two senior members of the crew. Here's Randy:

"You know, when you're watching the show it's cool and stuff, and it looks like great fun. But when they called and said come down and do this, I thought, you know, I've got to go and probably work five straight twelve-hour days

for tools that I don't really need. I got down here and, yeah, you do work hard for five days. I'm dragging now."

For John, who had plans for things to do in his spare time, the schedule is a bit more than he'd counted on:

"I thought I'd come out here and see a little bit of Long Beach, a little bit of California. Well, I know the ten blocks really good between here and the hotel. I really didn't think that we would work as hard, or as many hours, as we have. The car that we're doing has been really complicated. When I got up this morning my whole body was going, 'This isn't fun.' If I was working for the police department, I would have called in sick."

On Day Six it is time for the final test—time, that is, to make the donuts. Will they taste, or even look, like donuts? Will the crew that built the mobile donut shop eat whatever it is that comes off the end of the conveyor belt, especially after a build week that includes dozens of donut freebies?

"You betcha," John predicts. "I may have had enough donuts this week, but I'm certainly going to have one out of the car, that's for sure." John's enthusiasm for the product of their endeavors is not shared by all of his comrades, including Mike. "I'll at least bite into one," he says. "I've never eaten donuts every day for five days. I don't want to see any donuts for about a month." Randy is just as certain: "Not out of that machine. Well, I might have, like, one ceremonial bite." Even Jesse needs some convincing. "I don't want to eat a donut," he says, "out of anything that was pumped through a tube that was made in Monster Garage."

The donuts are made. They come rolling off the conveyor looking ready for your local donut shop. How do they taste? Check your television listings, turn it on, tune it in, and check it out. ⚙

FASTEN YOUR SEAT BELTS FOR A WILD RIDE :

INSIDE MONSTER GARAGE™

The ultimate backstage pass to the garage where host Jesse James, along with great gearheads from coast-to-coast, turn ordinary cars into extraordinary machines.

Exclusive behind-the-scenes photos, interviews, and stories uncover everything about the skills, the thrills, and the drama of more than 20 vehicle transformations.

PLUS: IN-DEPTH VEHICLE SPECS

BEFORE-AND-AFTER PHOTOS

OTHER TRANSFORMED VEHICLES FROM PAST AND PRESENT

THE MEN AND WOMEN WHO PRODUCE MONSTER GARAGE

FIVE DAYS.
3,000 BUCKS.
"CAN'T DO THAT" IS NOT AN OPTION.

LET THE SPARKS FLY.

Bonus 14 x 20-inch pull-out poster of host Jesse James